POSSERILLA

A TIME FOR TOMAHAWKS

BY

CLAWSON SMITH

No one rides alone.

INTRO:
LOST AND FOUND

A year ago exactly I found myself deep in the devil's territory; a red graveyard of fossil-riddled hoodoos in the high desert. I came to be lost. Instead, I was baptized in the devil's bathtub. Do not repeat what I have—it is magic reserved only for psychos, a PVP mode for fighting inner demons.

With a bad attitude and a gut full of psilocybin—having conducted a 48 hour fast to dedicate my flesh to the 3-threaded mysteries that I broke on top of a mesa, visited by twin ravens—I began my roam on a hunch I'd learn something. I broke my rule; never ask questions on a spirit journey. Immediately the heat and lack of water hit my frontal lobe with a sledge. Architecture of silt and stone began to transform around me with horrific speed. Gigantic boulders transformed into grinning skulls, hoodoos into femurs and bones clawing from the earth's core. I saw other hikers who transformed ghoulishly, walking and talking into the retarded wails. Walls melted around me and the ancient desert swallowed me whole.

Have you ever heard of the rare effect mushrooms have where you go into a 'time-loop'? I was on a Hero's Journey amount of the substance by the way, inheriting the masochism of shamans—to where you begin to repeat your experience over and over? Where trails go round and round and round? Where deep down you know you're never getting out of the trip? This was my journey. I was sentenced to a lifetime under the midday sun. I had become *draugr*—in Old Norse the true meaning the 'again-walker' to literally be a being condemned to endless and meaningless wandering, with a cursed soul.

Because I had come here to ask the gods and Fate

what my path should be; I was drawing a blank on life. I didn't know what my path was. Drawn by the internal magnetism in my blood, I came to demand the ancients what I should do for my career, my location, and my future. You can imagine how down I was, the dark places my mind went to when I was sucked into that zombie shadow desert and cast like a rotten bone into the hole. Initially. I was lower than a snake's belly in the Draugr Vision.

How very wrong I was.

Some brief backstory; the night previous my companions camped nearby and I slept in the open bed of my old Toyota pickup under the glare of the full moon. In the early luminescent morning I was awoken as a whole gang of coyotes circled my truck—and I mean they came so close that without my contacts I could still make out their triangle faces. And they didn't howl or yip but merely danced around my camp with their gold-gray coats like midnight messengers, running right up to my truck. Then they scampered off into the arroyo moat that surrounded the valley of demons, yipping and howling at the lunar oracle.

As soon as I returned to camp I was spurned by the comedown after I finally digested the mushrooms known as the 'glow' to some, I realized the visitation of the coyote had not been accidental. I was overcome with an awakening impulse to follow their trail—despite the fact the hard clay bore no signs or marks by the ghostly dogs. Tearing off my sandals I began to walk into that radiant afternoon sun—where greenery blossomed still in the bones of where a great river once flowed. Hunting for tracks that were not there. But they were; an astonishing lupine print was right there in the clay.

Squatting there in the vast riverbed and scratching my head, I began to ponder; why was my Draugr Vision so hellish, bookended before and after by this gang of coyotes. For a moment I foolishly considered it was a sign from Ullr that I needed to pick up a career in hunting—I'd planned to go in search for elk that fall and was determined to hew my way into the Alaskan frontier. That dissipated and suddenly I was struck, blindsided by my stupidity! I was a fucking moron to not have seen it before!

The Draugr Vision was brutal and alien in its delivery but instrumental in teaching me that my future would be barren if I was to walk in isolation. Meanwhile the trickster coyote, impish and sly but clever, were there taunting me as if to say "*Where is your gang? Where is your pack? Your people*?" ...and yet they left their tracks for me to follow. A heading if you will.

That trip precipitated what I am about to tell you.

Let's just cut right down to the bone—no foreplay or ass-squeezing. Do you think you squandered your youth by the shadow of danger that haunted your adventures? Or did you squeeze the pulp out of life, living on razor's edge of vido los barbaros? When your eyes open every morning, do you worry if you will live to see another sunrise as a slave to a system? Would you prefer to go gonzo with stillettos and duel your enemy for a chance of a life free of blood debts, or would you prefer to 'rise and grind' the rest of your miserable life; taxxed, vaxxed, and chipped like a wet robot because you preferred the path of slavish peace?

Will you die alone?

¡La madre que te parió, amigo! By the gods how these last years have aged us like little avocados. When last I spoke in my previous work, our world had undergone a horrible mutation that was becoming nigh-unrecognizable. Now it's synthesized into a reality of pure chaos. I imagine by the time I reflect upon this work our current state affairs will resemble a ditch-pig rolling in the carcasses of social media influencers. After all fresh meat is now a luxury. People are selling shitty cartoons pictures online for more than unattainable houses, which are being bought en masse by corporate slumlords, leasing them to tenants who are broker than my aunt when she spent our family inheritance. Unfuckable harpies are being begged by men half their fat index to be unjustifiably ploughed—daily. Trains being derailed like its 1870 sans the shiny railway bonds while dams are being slotted for planned demolition because nobody can fix the damn things.

It's getting really ugly out there!

More and most importantly you have probably noticed the social shift—this Madness almost that is sweeping up the common folk you interact with on a daily basis who are increasingly hostile and prickly—eagerly awaiting the day to shed blood on behalf of their battered dignity and pride in whatever rights they are deluded into thinking they have left. You can taste the numb horror of loneliness and depravity in the air that seems to be subdued only by daily dopamine dumps about the newest and shiniest fad—even that loses its luster after the seven-minute attention mark. We've not yet hit terminal rot here in our comfortable plastic world and it already feels like we're stumbling aimlessly through a rotting carcass of what was once a great empire.

Almost like the draugr...yes?

Yes a great and dark Hunger is on the horizon for the first world humans; you are staring at it. On the brink of a Great and Terrible Winter—our modern day Ragnarok—approaches which has been abated only by greed inherited by our forefathers. This era of financial flowering is at its close! If we are to selectively trust the annals of antiquity then what looms on the horizon is a series of collapses, revolutions, and civil wars that will leave every one of us shellshocked and even longing back for the luxuries we have today.

And. The. Lonely. Will. Not. Survive.

Full disclosure; when I came out with my first book of this sort of 'hooligan teeth-kicking youth memoir', I did not think I'd return to the writer's desk. I wanted to be done the internet and writing. My initial goal was to venture into Outer Mongolia die on the howling steppe. I was done. My stomach soured in too short of time after my last book after dealing with grifters, identity salesmen, and the general feeding frenzy of maggots who call themselves 'content creators'. Brick my skull! Those human larvae and their regurgitated 'masculinity' pretending to have the answer by merely ingesting liver—so help me that they are shielded by the law and murder is frowned upon. I told you I was working on a sequel but in reality I had a few sentences ripped from book numero uno that I cobbled together into a spiritual manifesto and what did I really want to do? Put a bullet into my laptop and maybe a few skulls, fill up some gas tanks, and truck it into the deep wilderness to live as a fugitive without ever hearing one more thing about 'internet culture'.

Well as you can tell, that didn't pan out. My traveling and engaging with my peers in the two years opened my eyes to what's been sprouting up from Nebraska to Manhattan—this depraved and hyper-socialized Madness everywhere—fermenting a gut-wrenching realization that we are imminently hurdling towards the precipice of societal immolation. The year of the Big Rat 2020 only confirmed to me that my previous assessments of 'the adults in charge' was clear; our world is run by idiot-chickens with their heads cut off and all the infrastructure of the early West is rotten and falling into the sea. But these last years? Cowardice runs too deep in the bones of this dying culture—right to the marrow. Our fathers and grandfathers have left us out in the blizzard. Our generational reward is the boomer's hubris.

Today systematic handcuffs are being placed on men around me, sterility-serums shoved into their veins and all autonomy is forfeited for its inherent danger and yet for all these daily tyrannies where are our leaders? Where are our vanguards to counter these revolutionary crowds, these leftist modern Jacobins? Where is our Caesar? I open my eyes wide to behold the barren shambles of 'movements' and ideological preachers behind pulpits of self-help pamphlets urging all but especially the white, male, and angry American men to simply pay higher dividends to the Church of Guilt Racketeering while their civilization is razed behind underneath them by an ever-swelling horde demanding the flesh of the Heritage Peoples.

Which was what stilled my decision to leave you behind, dear reader. It was that so many asked into the void where their deliverance would come from. Their lack of purpose. Like wolves raised in a kennel and released into an alien grassland, their instincts subdued and their teeth sanded down to stumps.

"*Where are our leaders? Who will lead the wagon train?*" I heard my kinsmen scream with blood streaming down their shining cheeks, drowning out the gurus and their platitudes. They were axes without handles. Braves without chiefs.

One would say this is the mythos of our time or the flavor of our epoch; one of solitary desecration of the meritocratic man and then the psychotic revolutionary masses baying for blood. The mismanagement of our civilization leading to the utter neglect of leadership, cultivating into a very unromantic end to the luxurious existence we both were suckled on.

Extreme times call for extreme solutions.

It has occurred to me in reflection that the natural, gradual progression of the Goon is not one of '*Another 12 Rules To Kick Teeth In for Individualists*' because the lone Goon will bleed out on a hillside, a knee placed between his shoulder blades and forcibly injected with Gay Serum by a dozen obese police, ending up as gruel-eating chattel or dead if they're so lucky. That the works of these grifter nobodies looking for a quick buck are banking on your stupidity with their dopey gutter-oil guides on 'Preparedness' by regurgitating Marcus Aurelius—these will not staves off the Wolves of Winter. Nor will this kind of individualistic mentality! As history shows that ALL GREAT MOMENTS ARE CONDUCTED BY A HORDE, A CROWD, AND POPULUS!

This is your official disclaimer; my agreement to return to write is not to give advice on lifestyle and etiquette as the barbarians are at the gates—no, I breathe all the visceral WRATH into this tome—detailing the Age of Madness and the Atomized Man into a hyper-focused sulphur-riddled spell of thermal gravity that will chisel a new Goon to crush and pulp the former. A pagan promise to forge something eternal, something that will *last*.

Goonhood? Read it? Good. It's a spiritual filter and litmus test to see if your compadres are psychological knuckle-draggers or they get the memo. Other than that I don't plan on rehashing the same points in my former book unless they're pertinent to the conversation. It is pointless to tell you to go outdoors when the price of a meal-loaf is higher than your mortgage. Or when you have no other soul to turn to when the knives fly.

Time is simply no longer a luxury we have.

Decades from now perhaps I'll write a five-installment 1000-word monstrosity waxing on the finer points of Biological Communism and uninstalling our inferior's intestines through sheer wit alone. On that day my children's children will be dining on buttered biscuits and breast milk with silk gloves and we'll all laugh like jolly fellows about how dreadful the Kali Yuga was like the aristocratic Saxons we are. Not today—today is the day of the Dane. Scalps instead of buttered biscuits and blood oaths traded for cheery platitudes. And the gloves stay off.

Now to the point.

Besides wearing a Mjolnir you made from scrap iron and becoming a roided-out barbarous fiend who can fend off five Pinko thugs behind the local diner during the impending hunger riots, you need to start thinking about man's best friend—and it ain't Fido. It's your fellow banditos who show up to throw hands with the urban Americans who try to head-canoe you while you went to take a piss after they robbed the convenience store for Benadryl and Cheetos.

I speak of the posse. The warband. The Mannerbund. The ride-or-die Goons. Your bloodmad brothers.

You asked for it. You wanted to learn how. Here goes nothin.

Sooner than you'd like you're going to need chiefs and lords like you need air. We're on the verge of a flaming reckoning of fire and brimstone and the men who will come out of this spiritual dark age will ride like the Devil's own Apaches—a pagan horde like hundreds more of ruthless savages laying waste to the fetid remainder of greater empires, engorging themselves on the stringy meat of what was once the Beast of the West. An apocalyptic cannibalistic feast that will turn our world inside out. It's not a moral conquest—penitent better have shotguns next to their bibles because your god (or gods) will not save you. Violence will be a currency in abundance.

And if you're not joining a gang you better be starting one.

This entire book could be detailing how the game is rigged. I could paint a grim dystopia of our monolithic cyberpunk dystopia like so many of my dissident colleagues—boring and too doomy. There are many talented writers who have done an eloquent job of this already. I could wield the great Hammer of Rhetoric—like my enemies do, and far too often—instead of *speaking of concrete action.*

What I mean to say is if you stick around a casino long enough your shit smells like cigars and the ambient roll of a dice never stops bouncing in your skull. You don't have a choice whether you become entrapped by the psychosis; it's part and parcel the day we live in, frendo. You can't simply facts and logic yourself out of this cancer with any amount of stoicism. Or individualism in a time of tribalism. This is coping and philosophical rabbit food. Big fucking surprise it doesn't fill you up.

My advice is you don't eat.

I opened my previous book **GOONHOOD** with: "*what gods do you pray to?*" and in the days since, I have recognized what I was tapping into wasn't merely provoking a shallow rote but an invoking word sorcery that stirred a transcendent, upward spirit of a Primitive Frontier Warrior Cult that would make Butch Cassidy and Genghis proud. Because it's exactly what we need. It's an uncomfortable subject to many of the 'Heritage Americans' (aka WASP and Germanic peoples who settled the frontier) but this spirit is what precedes that 'culture' which many of our modern peers deny exists and yet cling desperately to whatever reminds them of the Anglo foundation of this country—powdered wigs and all.

Nepotism beats despotism, aces high. Loners die lonely. Nature's most successful are those work in concert; the wolfpack, the eagle pair, the herd of bison. Historically small warbands and gangs of men have always thumped the individual powerhouse. Special forces today is structured in tight-knit teams who are individually specialized yet bred to be an adaptive fighting force capable of heroic, inhuman achievements. On their own they are king Goons on their own—barbarians fully autonomous to whack and kneecap like any primitive brute with the support of the infrastructure morass of Uncle Sam. But as a team? An unstoppable force.

Play your cards right and at the end of this game you'll number among such a posse of scalp-takers when the dawn of the new age bleeds a violent meridian. And I mean that in all sincerity—THERE IS NO SAVING, THERE IS NO RETURNING, THERE IS NO SENTIMENT. TURN YE BACK FOOLS IF YE WANT HOPE-PORN.

"IT (THE SYSTEM) GIVES THOSE WHO HAVE BEEN SUBMITTED TO IT A VIOLENT DISLIKE TO THE STATE OF LIFE IN WHICH THEY WERE BORN, AND AN INTENSE DESIRE TO ESCAPE FROM IT. THE WORKING MAN NO LONGER WISHES TO REMAIN A WORKING MAN, OR THE PEASANT TO CONTINUE A PEASANT, WHILE THE MOST HUMBLE MEMBERS OF THE MIDDLE CLASSES ADMIT OF NO POSSIBLE CAREER FOR THEIR SONS EXCEPT THAT OF STATE-PAID FUNCTIONARIES. INSTEAD OF PREPARING MEN FOR LIFE FRENCH SCHOOLS SOLELY PREPARE THEM TO OCCUPY PUBLIC

FUNCTIONS, IN WHICH SUCCESS CAN BE ATTAINED WITHOUT ANY NECESSITY FOR SELF-DIRECTION OR THE EXHIBITION OF THE LEAST GLIMMER OF PERSONAL INITIATIVE. AT THE BOTTOM OF THE SOCIAL LADDER THE SYSTEM CREATES AN ARMY OF PROLETARIANS DISCONTENTED WITH THEIR LOT AND ALWAYS READY TO REVOLT, WHILE AT THE SUMMIT IT BRINGS INTO BEING A FRIVOLOUS BOURGEOISIE, AT ONCE SCEPTICAL AND CREDULOUS, HAVING A SUPERSTITIOUS CONFIDENCE IN THE STATE, WHOM IT REGARDS AS A SORT OF PROVIDENCE, BUT WITHOUT FORGETTING TO DISPLAY TOWARDS IT A CEASELESS HOSTILITY, ALWAYS LAYING ITS OWN FAULTS TO THE DOOR OF THE GOVERNMENT, AND INCAPABLE OF THE LEAST ENTERPRISE WITHOUT THE INTERVENTION OF THE AUTHORITIES."

I quote lengthily Gustav LeBon because I cannot even afford to dive into the meat of this book before prefacing it with this; the playbook of our enemy goes back to Napoleon and perhaps earlier, but they have perfected in the 18th, the 19th, and 20th century this MKULTRA control over the populace—like an octopus wielding social pressures and depravity. Those banal needs, it merely stretches a tendril out and sends a horde of drug-addicted trannisaries to mass r*pe children of delusional, detached parents.

These are barely humanoids that we are facing, creatures created by a secular, anti-mythological group that sucks life out like a vacuum and tries to disrupt any organic organization outside The System. They are actively trying to whitewash all of history and to rewrite it in their own image. But this is also a massive undertaking and people today are inordinately stupid pig-people doped up on industrial solvent and cartoons, which is why you and I can see it happening clear as day. Back in LeBon's time such an attack on French antiquity and tradition was remarkably new (and coincidentally only happened when Askhenazi revolutionaries were allowed in the country again) but I digress...

If you were paying attention to the mass media endorsed violence and tyranny in the streets of 2020—when the banker-Jacobins flexed their fingers and loosed the massified swarm of Negroid-Leninists behind the veneer of social equality and reparations—did you felt the pressure? Did you feel isolated? Did you realize all the talking heads had nothing but sugar pills to feed you while the cities were put to the torch? Did you also notice how on every video the Bantu were milling about, kicking rocks and muttering gibberish under the breath until pseudo-whites came to direct them with flags and airhorns?! Yes you might have wondered why these 'liberated' people needed direction from their former masters like their kindred on the Mother continent did during the Communist Campaigns of Rhodesia.

Make no mistake; this was a coordinated REVOLUTIONARY call to arms, a lighting of the beacon reminiscent of early and darker ages of mass demonstrations and manipulation of the hungry and desperate as in LeBon's time. What you might say is the true purpose of democracy; wielding the rat horde. Because socialist revolutions are not rational or intellectual—they are cannibalistic and greedy and driven COMPLETELY by a religious fervor. And we are about to witness one.

Record high inflation and supply chain shortages can be solved quick term but these solutions will not stem the cultural rot and pitting of the Anglosphere's bones. Prisons are being emptied as we speak in Cuckafornia while the media ramps up the call for 'Reparations' and political trials for dissidents of a supposed 'Insurrection'—aka loosing the rabid wolves upon the Anglo/Germanic Middle Class of founding American stock—do you think you can withstand that tide of blood and brine that will come with the crime sprees of the next decade? Our history is defined by the days that gold was smelted into the pommels for swords and ivory for the handles of pistols, not vice versa. Whether it's these nerds and their psychological games or it leaping onto foreign sands to lay the hate on some cannibal savages, the outcome is the same.

Blood is in the water.

So I must repeat with total zeal that this work is NOT OF THINK-MASTURBATION AND IDEOLOGY, it is about preparing for the Great and Wild Hunt! It *is* man's true and oldest friend; the warband, the Mannerbund, the posse!

This is the spiritual successor to **GOONHOOD** because it is the maturation of rebellious boys into the triumphant, rallying cry of vitality—of determined men bound together not by fear of death but by the call of Life and Danger. It is the pagan spirit of Danes preparing to go 'on the viking' that is connected by glory and action—the manifestation of divinity! It is the natural reaction to man who knows his enemy wishes to subdue him, salt his lands, and tear down his monuments.

No war can be without its mythology and yet neither can mere myth guide you to victory. THIS is why the Boomer 'bootstraps' mentality in wake of the Covid Lockdowns, revolutionary riots, and the leftoid wave has seen no resistance! There is no mythos! No story of counter-revolutionary victory or historical figures to idealize besides wig-wearing Anglos who couldn't even agree on what kind of mercantile empire they would start! And even then the American Revolution was entirely white, entirely liberal, and entirely of its Time.

We are not of that Time.

Despite the name do NOT assume this is a book on guerilla-isms and revolutionary idealism—that's for the depraved junkie Flea whose flesh and mind is the pawn for the 'climate of revolution' as Che puts it. Goons might be inclined to even agree with the revolutionary spirit—even empathize with the underdog plight of The Flea at points but only because he loathes his plastic masters. So I quote the self-contradictory and communist-sympathizer Robert Taber;

"THE GUERRILLA FIGHTER IS PRIMARILY A PROPAGANDIST, AN AGITATOR, A DISSEMINATOR OF THE REVOLUTIONARY IDEA, WHO USES THE STRUGGLE ITSELF-THE ACTUAL PHYSICAL CONFLICT-AS AN INSTRUMENT OF AGITATION. HIS PRIMARY GOAL IS TO RAISE THE LEVEL OF REVOLUTIONARY ANTICIPATION, AND THEN OF POPULAR PARTICIPATION, TO THE CRISIS POINT AT WHICH THE REVOLUTION BECOMES GENERAL THROUGHOUT THE COUNTRY AND THE PEOPLE IN THEIR MASSES CARRY OUT THE FINAL TASK-THE DESTRUCTION OF THE EXISTING ORDER AND (OFTEN BUT NOT ALWAYS) OF THE ARMY THAT DEFENDS IT."

As many of my anonymous frends online are so apt and keyed-in to understand, the guerilla agitprop and this 'Anarcho-Tyranny' we have seen by black block groups and government is funded by alien Pharisees. No guerilla acts completely for the will of the people—that's monkey brained. Anarchist and communist goblinoids (I touch on this later) will be financed to subvert and corrupt the populace for the gain of international gangs, not so bread is cheaper and everyone can live a carefree life in the woods.

We—the anti-guerilla guerilla Goons—are seeking power through organized mobs...

...For our peaceful future backyard barbecues of course! I am merely a funny meat-cooking man who likes to talk in these strange hypotheticals which cannot be taken as serious advice anyway...

I am the Law without the Sea; an inland privateer, Mormon Medici, and entertainer! I lean heavily upon my background of friend-making, networking and industriousness whom only the offspring of pioneers have mastered. Though I am no son of Yaweh any longer I have keenly noted how tribal my fellow magic-underwear kinsman are and the social implements they have used to construct a social empire. Along with my feral instincts, a love for violence and the imprints of wild gods tattooed onto my skull from the ancient and naked lands, I have pieced together what I believe will bear the fruits of tribal prosperity.

My oath to you is that this book will be comedically practical. I sign this in my own blood—my living integrity—that it should not be anything less. These are anecdotes I would not give out unless I chewed on them every morning. These are lessons I have picked up on from building several networks of men; be them surrogate males totally useless in the realm of survival or fellow grit-eaters who strode with me in the deep wilderness and laughed at the idea of hypothermia in a blizzard.

In days to come when you walk into civilization and must participate with the Maddened and their addiction to tyranny—in case you're wondering, yes this is a trait of immigrants to an empire, swearing allegiance to the strongest bidder, which in the West means Non-White—so you should think of how many axes you will need at your side. How many fellow Goons that will stand shoulder to shoulder—prepared to face the maelstrom. What material should this warband be made of? How many? Will they break or will they hold? How can you trust them? Will they be enough?

Truthfully these cannot be answered until the day comes when you and your Goonsquad are faced with the revolutionary meatgrinder—on that day I pray to the gods you are victorious. And on that day of tomahawks and blood, ask yourself the opening line of this book—I say with certainty you will wear a smile remembering when you had nothing; no warband, no loyalty, no eyes to behold your glorious end and pass it on for generations to come.

I give you the bones to build this foundation.

LIVE, LAUGH, LAUNCH A SUCCESSFUL COUNTERATTACK UPON THE SEETHING MASSES. SCALP SOME SCUM. YOU MUST BECOME THE HYBIRD OF A MILK-DRINKING BARBARIAN AND A SHREWD CHARLATAN. THIS IS A POSSE PHILOSOPHY ROBBING GUERILLAS OF THEIR RADICAL ATTITUDE AND RESOURCEFUL STYLE.

POSSERILLA.

HERDING CATS

"A small lake has a little sand.
The minds of men are small
and not all men are equally wise.
No man is whole." ~ Havamal

Say tomorrow you're in Generic Semi-Urban Location minding your own business when you're alerted to the wondrous symphony of the sound of your Smart Clownmobile windows being smashed in by the wonderful migrant boys from down the hallway. They're turning your Japanese junker into a Kinder egg so they can get to the creamy middle; your wallet, your laptop, and other valuable property. You can't call the cops because they stopped answering calls regarding the, uh, Diverse and Indigenous Peoples....unless you happen to be a taxpayer who says the naughty racist words or your Virus DNA ID card is out of date because you can't afford this month's anti Airborne-AIDS booster. Then you're boned.

Your options are to a) let the robbing happen or b) try to intervene. Except there's three of them and one of you. Using a gun is out of the option—whether you're allowed to own one or you're already a Goon-certified rule breaker in a cucked country—because you'll be raked over the coals of the Racial Equity Commissars and using a gun is suicide by prison. On the up and up; the cops aren't coming anyway because they're more worried about losing their jobs to said Racial Equity Commissars.

You, still having testicles, go with option B. However in this very fabricated and totally fictional scenario, you don't want to go 3v1 because you're not 6'4", 250 lbs Muay Thai monster cycling 750mg Trenbolone acetate a week kind of confident in your people-breaking skills.

You need backup.

Here's the kicker; who do you call? Who do you know is going to show up—and if need be, actually go toe to toe with these thugs by your side? Write down the names of these compadres of yours and on a scale from 1-10 how willing they would be to commit acts of ~~violent impunity~~ conflict resolution with you. How many are there? Ten? Five? Two? One? Or are your friends all of the lobotomites who are too busy stuffing their faces with temporal vulturism and too afraid to act out for fear of reprisal and societal cancellation?

If you're the poor sucker who just wrote a black zero then maybe option A is the practical route—it's also the cowardly route and it sucks. And it's a wakeup call; you are byproduct of a decadent grain-based empire descended from a pastoral frontier colony whose intent is to maintain Power over you by keeping you fat, alone, and weak. What you need to realize is there is no ideology nor political solution that will revitalize the poisoned earth beneath you that provided bounty to the hunter-gatherer lifestyle or the 'culture' of those who sunk their teeth into the wild New World before it was industrialized. Slave populations will be sicced on the descendants of the founding peoples (European Whites) in exchange for calories, shiny things, or simply to keep the founding peoples as Non-Combatants and compliant.

All men are crowds. No man is free from his collective society exempting hermit pariahs who mythologically are allowed to return only when they have learned the Big Thing—some kind of divine reward of wisdom. As crude as it is a group of trading card enthusiasts or perhaps a Boomer fanclub of painted fire hydrants are considered a crowd. By definition this obsession of 'the thing' I believe is rooted in our survival mechanism of small Ice Age hunter tribes spreading out and needing to diversify their palette. X sub-tribe is overhunting mammoth so other X sub-tribe forms a hunting party and enjoys hunting big birds instead. Just replace birds and mammoths with hydrants and paper cards.

Whenever someone says that a man is MIGHTY it means he has sovereignty over his environment (a Goon, a cultured thug)—if it is said a man has POWER this means he has CROWD CONTROL. He can lead and deploy Man—whether man is by default a herd beast and follower—who is by far the most intelligent and godlike being on our mortal plane. Power and its ascendant value is why I mention Gandhi, Hitler, Jesus, Genghis as being in their category of uber-human demigods who are known purely by this mystical and gravitational charisma—unlike say a Baboon Obambo who has no raw Power as a stateman or even as a conductor and relies entirely on Kabbalah journalistic theater gimmicks to make him appear likeable or a figure of influence. I laugh at the idea that Virginian warrior caste went abroad to find mountain-dwelling genocidal Towelhead because some racially ambiguous Commie faggot like Obambo waved his scepter. You should too!

Yes I state and dare any to disprove that raw Power over the Crowd is the supreme ruler over society and ideology is just an accessory to he who holds It.

I met a boomer kingpin who was disgustingly rich from building sales teams in the pharmaceutical industry—he has his own copyrighted program and the whole goofy bit. The kicker? He can't hire a crowd of jack-offs to sell a patch of free swampland to a Seminole. In other words; he hires a ditzy pair of tits to do his hiring process for him. His sales program I had the privilege of watching safely behind glass (to mercilessly laugh at) consisting of power point presentations of >HOW CAN I SELL MY SOUL AND PRECIOUS FREE SPIRIT TO THE PLASTIC CORPARATION WHEN I'M ALREADY SLEEPING AT MY DESK< or perhaps the out of touch >PULL YOURSELF UP BY THE BOOSTRAPS MILENNA-TURD, MY FATHER DIDN'T FIGHT IN TWO WORLD WARS SO YOU COULD TWEET ALL DAY< . And *he* got paid the big bucks.

Sad to say King Drugs is a dime a dozen in the post-Dot Com era. It's a depraved world out there when your boss actually listens to Jim Cramer unironically.

Recruiting isn't sales and you can teach a monkey how to bargain his bananas. Finding people, learning their strengths and weaknesses, harnessing your inner Danny Ocean by building a team of reliable people isn't easy—it's a lost and delicate art. You know how in the movies the heist crew always has the right people who can jiggle a lockpick under the pressure of police sirens and an impending lifetime in jail? That's Hollywood. There's a reason why an overwhelming majority of small businesses fail and often; they hire the wrong people with the wrongly shaped skulls. How you can shoot yourself in the foot in the debut of your own Goongang movie is to bring on a bunch of loose cannons, losers, and lazy sonsofbitches.

Back in the day if you needed a bunch of braves or good old boys to raid, you just waltzed out of your teepee and had your pick of the cream of the crop. But with atomization and decentralization of the suburban population, your task here will take a little bit more walking, talking, and even stalking to start your selection and recruiting process. You're also going to need to master subtlety because you can't exactly advertise that you're looking for Spiritual Mercenaries Capable of Deadly Acts Who Will Marry Your Sister via your local newspaper or on the HOA corkboard. However, if you say

Weekend Men's Cardplaying Club @ Jack's House BYOB & Snacks, you can get away with advertising murder without being put on a watchlist (a second one because you already are if you bought this book).

No I intend literally; start an exclusive poker club and buy cheap beer to pass around. No hot-blooded male will turn that down. Just make sure you're not playing with cash (you'll turn more strangers into enemies faster than if you asked who their favorite sports teams were). Yeah poker comes up a lot—follow this book down its natural course you'll see that Hold 'Em is my favorite; sue me faggot.

Ultimately it boils down to your ability to make the greatest number of acquaintances, who you can then filter out for quality using a number of psychological tests—more on that later—and then be left with some candidates who have fertile minds for dissidence, then eventually form micro-societies. Oh many mafias started this way. The trick here is knowing where to be to recruit—i.e. location, location, location—knowing some basic social skills, and a little dash of revolutionary luck. Your time would be much better spent in say, a martial arts gym where people are already accepting that natural hierarchies exist, rather than attempting to forcefeed the idea of piratical warlordism to the local pottery club who are currently sculpting reparation busts in honor of Saint George Floyd.

Sporadically and with a little luck you might run into a fellow at the laundry mat or at the grocery store who doesn't lap up dogshit and digs your tune—this is why we prepare our salespitch in the shower mirror gentlemen.

A car salesman and a spook are sitting at the hotel bar and polish their drinks. The Dominican bartender fills them up and then asks the spook, *"So what do you do for work senor?"*

Being pretty toasted, he smugly replies "*HUMINT. That means I'm basically a spy and manipulator who knows how to torture and extract intel from people by masterful psychology techniques.*"

"*Very nice very nice senor. Can you prove it?*"

So the spook pulled out his CIA badge.

The bartender nodded and turned to the car salesman, "*And what about you senor?*"

The car salesman says, "*First, I noticed a VW rabbit outside. She yours?*"

"*Si si!*"

"*You know the repairs on that thing are going to cost you more than getting a new one primo? And I couldn't help but notice the custom exhaust and racing tires. Have you ever thought about a turbo Jetta? Why drive a dogshit car when I can get you something slick for pennies on the dollar...*"

The night grew late and the whiskey bottle empties. The two men went their separate ways; one who was a manipulator who knew how to torture and extract intel from people by masterful mind techniques. The other was a CIA spook.

Being a cutthroat salesman is in fact a rarity in this modern time and the art of sales and social manipulation is like speaking fluent Latin. There are no salesman in the world of Merchants now—just soft-handed gigolos with overmanicured beards and patterned shirts who are Shabbos goy for the Ashkies on Wall Street. These 'salesmen' are Nordstrom-wearing hermaphroditic morons who on paper might have money but they are house-poor and couldn't sell you the breakfast slams at Dennys if they were chewing on the barrel of a .44.

In the Age of the Merchants how is this so? Simple;

when you achieve total monopoly of the market (i.e. Ashkies kicking out Anglos and Dutch and turning America into their own personal financial empire) you lose the ability to fight tooth and nail for personal wealth. You lack any hunger and drive. Your only aspiration in life is to speed run your career into becoming a Tesla-driving faggot. Honestly have you ever asked yourself how many of these yuppie skinsuits have been so poor they opted to buy Ramen instead of toilet paper for the month? I'll answer that for you; big fucking zero. Sales isn't a jungle like it was in 1932. It's a giant guinea hamster wheel dangling dopamine cheese bits in front of gullible rodent-minded people—just keep those stubby little feet propelling the wheel to feed the international financial monster!

Sterility, safety, and stability. That's why you don't have salespeople or their word-sorcery on display anymore. You won't find a Wolf of Wall Street or a Mad 'Ad' Man anywhere in New York because that creates unnecessary risk that endangers the total homogenization of the (purely speculative) market that governs our day to day. When you break it down you realize that finance is just shadow games and sales is just being clever/charismatic/charming enough to socially dominate another. And because everything is about owning the transaction versus the product, it hurts the System when you have little one-off independent guys who understand how sales works and chew off even 1% of any profit. Why the Wolf of Wall Street got nabbed by the way.

1% of America's Economy is an astronomical number of pure Monopoly money that is layered under devious algorithms of invisible speculation and bloated, entirely fictitious systems (quantitative rectum loosening) that no one man actually understands—like an ever-increasing

1000+ word safe combination that's micromanaged by multiple countries to prevent any thievery from occurring. One salesman may seem miniscule to this bloated behemoth but then again Henry Ford was only industrialist and he upended the entire economy in a very short period.

I don't want to get in the weeds of the metaphysics of markets as I'm sure that's not what you came here for, but when you understand that money is just representative of human capital—social energy in simple terms—everything becomes a whole lot clearer why things are so homogenized and why it's crucial to keep anything from rocking the boat.

You may not be cut out of the cloth of a Don Draper but you sure as hell can learn—I fucking did and I'm a mong who writes books. Door to door sales taught me something invaluable about manipulating people; everyone is a psychologically-fragile infant, all you need to learn is which button to push to get them to empty their wallet. That's it. Sales is just one big psycho-warfare where you are divining intel from people by throwing them curveball questions, following up with charm, and finishing them off with crude techniques like emotional gaslighting to get them to buy your product.

The best advice I ever got when I stepped into the gladiator pit of sales was this;

"MONEY IS A MAN'S MOST PRIZED POSESSION. HE KEEPS IT TUCKED IN HIS WALLET AND DARES YOU TO TAKE IT. ONCE YOU FIGURE OUT HOW TO MAKE A MAN PART WITH HIS MOST PRIZED POSESSION AND OPEN THAT WALLET, THE WORLD OPENS UP TO YOU."

In the Meatspace—the offline, real world—it's important to adopt a pragmatic lens in terms of how to develop a valuable and engaging pitch to your mark and knowing how to position yourself to attract a loyal follower; an atomized individual and dopamine-addicted nobody whose in the same sinking ship as you. Don't re-invent the wheel when formulating your recruiting message. You must understand what works and why it works. And what exactly, dearest and most fastidious reader, works?

Go and pirate yourself a copy of **HOW TO WIN FRIENDS AND INFLUENCE PEOPLE** before you get another page in this book here. It's not all overrated Boomer turds. It's critical. It's fundamental. It compliments if not overrides my own anecdotal ramblings of stumbling through social altercations. But most importantly it has some key ideas wherein you will find on what makes another lost soul tic—how you can become a human puppeteer to win yourself new friends—friends who are capable, have qualities you think would befit your own survival and they yours.

One absolutely gravitational lesson from Carnegie;

"AROUSE IN THE OTHER PERSON AN EAGER WANT."

Aka abuse the honey and spare the vinegar.

If you don't want to spend the time to read Carnegie's book, then heed this lesson above all; ordinary people DO NOT want to hear about your current dilemmas; why there are holes in your shoes, or why you can't make rent—they care about THEIR immediate issues like the selfish creatures they are. Men can be loyal, candid, and valiant brothers one day but every moment they're these qualities they're self bastards because they're all thinking *"how do I get my next steak/fuck/bed/piece of gold?"*. Women think similarly but with their nether regions, aka womb-brained. All social research confirms this by the way—fact check me at your misery.

This baseline of selfishness doesn't make Men bad—it makes them mortal, culpable, but also extremely easy to predict. Every guy who has a pulse has all these instincts, whether he's a coconut-harvester in Malaysia or a Bavarian bouncer. Which is exactly why the first arrow in your make-a-buddy quiver should be; *"I should find out what this fella wants and what is important to him so I can win him over to my side."*

Bingo.

So simple, so easy, a chimp with an extra chromosome could do it? And yet very few leaders even consider this—why? Because men don't depend on them. NCOs or sergeants in any military branch are considered 'personable' to their men because they know them best; their desires, fears, sins, and victories. A good NCO is prized by his subordinates because he is their leader—they have declared him so. Is it any wonder then in comparison the higher-ranked Commissioned Officer who spent the last four years in a college studying homoerotic Euro-Pop music theory that shows up to command is immediately treated like the scum of the earth? Not particularly.

One last smoking gun for your pitch; don't get desperate. Never, ever, EVER beg. Not once. You will not catch yourself saying the word 'please'—erase it from your vocabulary. Your secret gang is exclusive, it is proprietary and it is not available to almost anybody.

A good salesman never has to beg for business—business should always beg for a good salesman.

There is a darker path to manipulating the hearts of men that needs mentioning, if even to understand your enemy. Now I will proceed to quote Saul Alinsky—yes, that Saul Alinsky and I know Obambo was such a student of his—because I have a death wish by a future Right Wing deathsquad and for what it's worth, his points are valid to understand from both an enemy's perspective and how revolutionaries conduct their recruiting;

"TO ORGANIZE A COMMUNITY YOU MUST UNDERSTAND THAT IN A HIGHLY MOBILE, URBANIZED SOCIETY THE WORD 'COMMUNITY' MEANS COMMUNITY OF INTERESTS, NOT PHYSICAL COMMUNITY. THE EXCEPTIONS ARE ETHNIC GHETTOS WHERE SEGREGATION HAS RESULTED IN PHYSICAL COMMUNITIES THAT COINCIDE WITH THEIR COMMUNITY OF INTERESTS, OR, DURING POLITICAL CAMPAIGNS, POLITICAL DISTRICTS THAT ARE BASED ON GEOGRAPHICAL DEMARCATIONS. PEOPLE HUNGER FOR DRAMA AND ADVENTURE, FOR A BREATH OF LIFE IN A DREARY, DRAB EXISTENCE."

There is a compelling argument here why **RULES FOR RADICALS** was the bible of the guerilla commie throughout the latter 20th century and not the KJB. The effectiveness of this type of quasi-Marxist tactic was that it targeted members of varying racial and religious groups on the basis of their economic disposition and their DESIRE FOR REVENGE—especially as the established American Empire was no longer in a conflict with other civilization types and was turning inward on itself to harvest maximum resources. Revenge and Perceived Injustice are the greatest tools in a manipulator's belt, even if they have a small amount of charisma or power. Want someone to side with you? Convince them that they've been anally reamed by (insert group here) and that you have the ability to give them what they rightfully deserve!

I refer to another communist revolutionary on the topic, the troglodyte Trotsky;

"WHATEVER MORAL EUNUCHS AND PHARISEES MIGHT SAY...THE FEELING OF REVENGE HAS ITS RIGHT...WE [MUST] DIRECT ALL OUR STRENGTHS TOWARD A COLLECTIVE STRUGGLE AGAINST THIS CLASS STRUCTURE. THAT IS THE METHOD BY WHICH THE BURNING DESIRE FOR REVENGE CAN ACHIEVE ITS GREATEST MORAL SATISFACTION!"

Why sell a man a skill that will take a lifetime to foster with a sliver of chance of success to obtain a mansion versus planting the notion in his head like a black weed that the mansion instead was built by *his* ancestor's hands and each brick is rightfully his and all he needs to do is to take it by force in seconds? How many people go out and get rich because they resent their father for being poor? How many rockbrained females jabber on about how they can prove they can do a man's job and then end up a bitter professional? *Revenge sells.* Nobody thinks of themselves as the antagonist of a story—especially not the bloodthirsty revolutionaries and kingdom-robbers of early 20th century Russia posing as the Have-Nots. Replace the words bourgeoise and proletariat with master and slave—this simple dichotomy can be a total farce and still dupe people into murdering millions.

You understand now that why these socialist revolutions had momentum and surged in the last 200 years is that THEY SELL A BELIEVABLE MYTHOS, A RELIGIOUS STORY LIKE RAGTAG REBELLION OVERTHROW DARK CAPE GUY that tugs at a man's heartstrings. All they need is the economic circumstances and a crowd hostile enough to another—i.e. the Color Revolutions overthrowing colonial masters, and now the same sentiment in the United States.

"BUT IN REPUBLICS THERE IS A STRONGER VITALITY, A FIERCER HATRED, A KEENER THIRST

FOR REVENGE. THE MEMORY OF THEIR FORMER FREEDOM WILL NOT LET THEM REST; SO THAT THE SAFEST COURSE IS EITHER TO DESTROY THEM, OR TO GO AND LIVE IN THEM."

Take a wild guess at the founding event of a country Machiavelli just predicted; America. Every modern historian will tell you that the tea being thrown in the harbor after outrageous taxes and an indifferent king was the spark that lit the red, white, and blue revolution of 'classic liberalism'—those historians are bottom-feeders who probably pocket hotel shampoo bottles thinking they're kitschy. Fucking retards. What actually precipitated that glorious colonial rebellion was Britain not only kicking Americans into a frontier-bush meatgrinder—the Seven Years War, or the French-Indian War—where peasant militias were expected to fight a superior Enemy, on His home turf, without proper arms or experience, but those crooked-tooth morons had the fucking audacity to charge those same American colonists a war-tax afterwards all while denying it was the bravery of Virginia boys that kept America from speaking French. In short? Americans wanted revenge and they got it.

Not that the meta or cause for this stranger you're talking to join should only pivot off of revenge, injustice, or discrimination one way or another—you name *them* the victim without them ever having to say it. This isn't a hard selling point since we're already living in a time where significant portions of our population are being declared domestic terrorists and enemies of the state. See you're planting a sense of inequity within them that would be subdued by their pride and stubborn sense to toil on! You are the airhorn to the Anglo-Saxon who slumbers on with his skull buried beneath a mountain of pillows—how rude of you, YOU very inconsiderate disturber of the peace, to awaken him! He was sleeping while his village was being plundered!

Now when you open here with your mark, even if it's a brief conversation, and make it memorable. You can earn this by simply empathizing with whatever mundane inconvenience this hypothetical recruit is bitching about that day. Landlord upping the rent because of Weimar inflation? Dog has herpes? Their girlfriend started an OnlyFans account? Just nod. Agree with them. This may seem too dumb, too baseline—it's not. Do you know how many people get complimented each day or have their grievances voiced? If they've gotten either, it's less than the fingers on their hand. Be that person who is there to hear them out and legitimize their bullshit.

Once in a harvest moon you strike out on someone who doesn't need your persuasion. These unicorns who already understand exactly what you're spitting and extend a friendly hand to shake yours—Ten Bulls and Jesse Wales style. Don't bank on it but count your roses when it does.

I went out several weekends ago to revel and I met one of these recruiting unicorns. A mutual acquaintance who showed up turned out to have a head on his shoulders; he knew Coof-SARS was a fraud, the vaxx is a cover for global super-surveillance networks and was listening to Independent Pundit to get all the radio chatter on The Next Big Political Thing. This kid was fairly athletic so we hit it off on jiu-jitsu, muay thai, etc. Not too many drinks in later we exchange numbers and now he's a member of the Goongang. What I didn't tell you is this kid was once a rabid socialist who was black-bloc-d up full-blown faggot until last November. A lucky exception to the rule!

One tactic to put in your verbal toolbelt is the age-old

slimeball journalist tactic; ask leading questions. Pay attention to their grievance-airing about gas prices or inflation and how the current president has a rotting cabbage for a brain and suggest something like: "*IF THESE LIBTURDS ARE JUST GONNA STEAL AN ELECTION DO YOU REALLY THINK THERE'S A PEACEFUL SOLUTION IF THEY'RE IMPRISONING INNOCENT PEOPLE WHO EVEN QUESTION THAT?*" Even if your mark disagrees with that question they're already accepting the rhetorical framework or story you've presented—this is exactly how the parasites of the Western Media Lie Industry—aka the news—convince people of a narrative without ever selling it to them!

Because the news has never been about truth; it's about selling a crafty story that tugs, steals, and chills people's souls. All you have to do is tell a better story than some beak-nosed hack who drinks craft kombucha.

Be most careful here, however. You do not want your mark to feel tricked or otherwise cheated. These are long-term relationships and friendships you are building with people. It's better to be blunt and have them trust you to always speak truth to power versus having them feel like some guinea pig or test subject! The Communists are ok with doing this because they have a track record of purging those who've served their purpose but may become a nuisance later on (Trotskyites and Ashkenazi assassins being turned to fertilizer by Stalin, for example).

Crude as these social tools may be we are fighting a disinformation war; our kinfolk and brothers are the victims of this Industrial System that uses pathological brainwashing and layers of lies to meld loyal slaves. Never forget this Evil Mammy Grain cult has corrupted them with this cancer and we should never feel guilty for doing what it necessary to heal our friend's minds.

Fertile as the hunting grounds for likeminds are, do not turn to social media, internet forums, or any kind of anonymous networks to recruit into your Goongang. As much as I am a devout fan of anonymity—as is just and your right, as everything that happens online is a shadow of reality—it is exceedingly difficult to maintain your OPSEC/PERSEC or compromise your offline compadres by doing this. Use common sense here. As was with the 'Plot to Kidnap a Governor' that occurred not to long ago and discovering almost every member save one man was a federal agent, it's a good rule of thumb to follow; don't fall into the Honeypot because it's convenient! Some are cleverer than others and as complex and intricate as dissident speech is online, your foe is catching up to your tricks. You're one DM away from landing yourself a spot in the future Guantanamo Gulag.

DO NOT RECRUIT ONLINE.

Are there exceptions to this rule? Yes, few, but still proceed with caution; these are mutual acquaintances you've either already met or a family member you or one of your Goongang trusts. It's much better to open up a line of communication offline or somewhere where the NSA isn't saving your messages and cold-storing them to build a dossier on your group of hilbilly Floridian Goons, aka the social media platforms. If all you have is a Faceborg or Instagrift or Twatter, keep it brief, vague and say something like 'let's meet up for coffee, here's my number, etc. etc.'.

A golden rule of thumb to follow on OPSEC/communication is; Would I send this to Grandma? Even if granny was in the IRA, this still applies!

Three places ripe for recruiting—lest you have your own—are really no surprise; gyms, clubs, and even churches. Being a heathen whose skin bursts into flame the moment I enter a building with a cross recommending churches may come as a surprise! But where else will you find such a saturation of fellows and ladies who already feel a sense of tribal unity, willing to sacrifice time every week, and are (likely) Christian in spirit and therefore chummy in some kind of Anglo Saxon way (note; if they're Irish Catholic and nationalist even better). Minus the mega-church televangelists, you will find brothers in arms in almost any House of the Lord today—and why shouldn't you? By being any combination of White, Christian, Middle-Class, and not lopping off your genitals is a crime if you turn on the news today! How many folk do you think are sitting in the pews every Sunday, watching their country deteriorate into a crumbling shadow and look from side to side, thinking; "*well maybe it is time to take up arms, but who would stand with me?*"

I would wager with every penny I make from this here troublesome little book that you'll amass quite a crew out of those good Saxon folk who still practice their Christian ways if you open with; "*Wasn't it those Bostonian boys who went to the same churches who took up arms against the British? Brothers I think it's high time we rekindled that tradition...*".

Gyms offer a different kind of asset—a man who prays at the feet of the Temple of Iron, manifesting a conviction in physical hierarchy and violence. This sort of spiritual brute is the backbone of your Goongang; the blue-collar man, the ex-Marine or off-duty fireman hitting the squat rack and the barbell. This man already believes our System is plagued by flabby, incontinent weakness—he sees it the moment he steps out into the public. These are mortal avatars of Thor even if they wear a cross upon their neck. Lift beside them and ye shall receive. And the best part? In a gym they are more often than not exceedingly if not *ridiculously* friendly.

First make it a priority to be a regular at this particular gym. Start then by making a passing comment or just nod in deference to these future Goons. Ask to use the machine or equipment after them. Offer to spot somebody if they look like they're going in on a three-plate bench. Compliment the brand of shirt they're wearing (the gift of a kind word, as you can already tell is a theme here). Make yourself known at this gym as being the kind of person who respects and will be respected. Your job is more than halfway done. So long as you maintain tact and show you are serious, these men will listen to what you have to say—blood respects blood.

(as an insert I also offer a sidebar; Polynesians who work as bouncers and muscle at bars are good goons. Their culture is ride-or-die. I have made a number of Hawaiian, Tongan, Samoan frends simply shaking their hand or hitting them up outside a bar to ask them if they have any good stories, how the bums are, etc. At some tequila bars I get 'priority' to skip the line by trading the Poly up front a gift card...you must start to think like this)

Lastly any other organizations or clubs. Unfortunately many of these male-focused or male-specific types of groups have been (intentionally) corrupted, destroyed, or otherwise rendered sterile by gynocritic car-bombs. This is why my insistence on using gyms is so critical; it is perhaps the last domain if any exist of a martial meritocracy—the natural and primitive foundation for any strong society—and your chances of finding common ground and an acceptable testosterone count will be far higher than say your local game store fandom fetishists! You might strike out a golden sombrero and find a gang of bodybuilders who play Warhammer 40k, but don't bet on it. You should prioritize and maximize your efforts where they'll be best received.

Mannsvit as it is referenced in the perennial and wise book, The Havamal, means to possess good sense or human understanding as opposed to being book-wise. The viking way of saying 'streetsmarts'. But this complex word is what I would call 'The Golden Eye' or having a keen sense of the inherent value in another's virtues. Right off the bat I don't expect you to be a master at reading somebody like some spook with a PhDick in shrinkology—your time is much wiser spent watching videos on this and skipping the student debt—but I do have some explicit suggestions to master the art of obtaining and honing your *mannsvit.*

Go out to town on a night, it can be fancy or shoestring. Pick a group, a couple, or just random individuals and start forming a story about their behavior towards one another. Analyze and predict their little mannerisms, if they make physical contact, where their bodies are facing, and whether they're laughing for starters. Girls are facing away from the guys or making little eye-contact? Somebody isn't getting some tonight. Are they hacking like hyenas every twenty seconds? Either they're hitting the Jamison hard or they're buds from way back when. What you're doing here is learning general body language tells by creating these stories. It doesn't matter if they're bullseye or bullshit—it's gaining that third eye for human intelligence that matters.

The second one is going to be difficult if you're a shut-in and turtle up when forced into social situations. You're going to need to learn how make people invested in your conversations—you might have all the AK-47s, private helicopters, and land on this side of the Mississippi to have an ~~effective counter-guerilla shock-cavalry when supply chains dry up~~ really fun hog-hunting side business, but it's jack-all if nobody likes talking to you.

Start asking engaging questions. Simple. Take the blandest small-talk topic you can think of; traffic, cars, clothing, weather. When asking somebody about it or stating a dumb, boilerplate comment follow it up with a hard 'why?' Instead of asking what somebody does, asking them why in Lucifer's salty taint they're a dog sitter—don't actually say this, but humor never hurts. They hate traffic? Ask them why they live here and not in BMFE where your only traffic are the cows who like to graze the fine weeds in the middle of the highway at 2AM. By digging deeper and asking the why to their behavior in a casual, friendly way, you are *making this person think you sincerely want to know them better* (suggestion; you actually should, if you plan on bringing them into your ~~polygamous steppe-compound~~ fun hog hunting business!). Also don't be fake about it and pay attention to what they say, because this is a perfect opportunity to use the Mirror technique (this works in sales like you wouldn't believe) to identify with something they're saying and springboard into a deeper conversation.

Mannsvit is more complex than your initial reading of a person but with testing the waters by simply vetting their body language or why they're a welder can give you a clearer picture on if somebody's worth trusting with your precious PERSEC. A good bladesmith understands that to achieve an apex in the sharpness of his knife, he must give it a good burr to work off of first! Any leader worth his grit is someone who can sense if his subordinates are worthy of his command, mannsvit—this good sense of the human and social element—will help him not only make the best selections for team members but know exactly what weaknesses his team possesses and so know the capabilities of his team.

Women aren't allowed in the club. There's a reason

why it's called a mannerbund and not a co-edbund or postsexualrevolutionbund, ok? I shouldn't have to spell this one out for you chief; women do not and cannot fathom the abstract concepts of 'honor' or 'loyalty' or 'patriotism'. Every single one of them is a Stockholm Syndrome bomb waiting to go (there's a reason why bride kidnapping was a common practice for tens of thousands of years by every tribal society across the globe). Women are explicitly and biologically loyal to one thing and one thing only, and it isn't spelled 'p-e-n-i-s'—it's spelled 'c-h-i-l-d-r-e-n'. Just because a woman can hit a bullet on a piece of paper does not preclude her most base and primitive impulse; to rear and protect her progeny. Men are disposable and our bargain with them is fairly one-sided as far as Nature is concerned.

Now is a woman a reliable asset to your mannerbund, your posse? Absolutely. I'm not saying the other (demonic) gender is to be shunned from your organization—merely that they are support characters, and they have a right to be. If you're married and have a mortgage, the woman has a right to know why you're spending your Saturdays in the freezing mud and why you're suddenly interested in the tactics of the Viet Cong. In the wise words of Clay Martin, "women have a predisposition for intelligence". Their gossipy natures are perfect for getting human intelligence—women are like spiders, spinning yarns and collecting little tidbits on their social web and farming little secrets from any fly that graces their silk.

Comparing females to Shelob aside, women do and should serve a critical function to the goongang; intelligence harvesting and cultivating your future pastoral compound, feeding your future sons breastmilk, etc. Keep them away from business.

Closing this out I have a few final remarks on just what kind of Joe or Jacques you're trying to bring onboard by using examples of my own Meatspace interactions and then recruiting to paint a clearer picture on what you might do.

Adam is a hiker, a former member of a military branch, and loves offroading. We started chatting about how grand a local mountain region was, thru-hiking, and hit it off as being similarly interested in survivalism. We went for a hike and figured out real quick we were on the same page about politics, preparation, and not Trusting the Plan. Adam didn't take any convincing because he was already looking for likeminded guys. He's a core guy and he shows up to every meet-up, not to mention his experience in the military is a major boon. He's a unicorn but I mention him because I would have never met Adam had I not jumped at the opportunity by opening the conversation with a similar interest in outdoorsmanship.

Jack is a total tech nerd and a programmer. He's a brother of another member who I met at one of those 'work-for-a-month-then-quit' jobs. Originally I invited him to just kick back and have some beers. I broached the subject of preparedness when he expressed concern (being the urbanite he is) at the riots and the sheer bedlam of 2020. By convincing him he needed a firearm and train with it to better defend himself, I was able to generate an interest in brotherhood in arms. By also combining training with inviting him to come lift weights with us, Jack has become a die-hard asset and is one of our most dedicated guys, despite being a computer-jockey.

Paul is a friend of one of our core guys. He's shown up twice to our trainings out of both being married and not being able to negotiate his way to a meeting without engaging in gladiatorial debates with said wife. He doesn't own a firearm or piece of equipment that we've put on our required list of gear. Paul is a pleasant man to talk to but having learned about his past, I've found out he would go months between jobs and live off unemployment because he found no motivation to work. Paul is a great example of somebody who seemed great skindeep until you got to be disappointed by him.

Tim is a notable mention because he was my first 'recruited' that wasn't a friend of a friend or family member or had anything in common besides meeting him at the local gun range. He hasn't shown up once to any of our get-togethers and I'd be shocked if he did. My getting him onboard was having a conversation about the general state of things politically and he agreed (begrudgingly) to join. I didn't read his body language but if I could go back in time, I bet you ten Comanche scalps the man wanted me out of his own.

Bjorn is the last example I'll give. He's just shy of flesh and blood, which makes us family. For the longest time he gabbed a storm about joining our group and becoming a real asset, a doorkicker. He, like the last two mentioned, is about as visible at our meetings as a cock on a cockroach. We don't spend much time together besides obligatory family gatherings and if I was a viking with a longship, he'd have an excuse to pick flowers in the meadow instead. I have stopped inviting him for my own sanity.

What is the uniting theme behind these six examples I've presented; activity and brotherhood outside the group. Adam and Jack are all the types of guys I try to spend time with on the weekends. As for Paul and Bjorn I've seen them less times this year than the inside of the same broad's apartment. Whether I'm putting any effort into spending time bonding is a fair critique on my part, but as for the others they reciprocate and invite me as much as I do them.

I've recruited dozens but only accumulated a clutch of Adams and Jacks. This isn't to discourage but present a realistic vision of what the fruits of your efforts might be if, say, you do as I did and cast a wide net over such a diverse and frankly unequal group. Numbers mean shit if you can't get at least one Adam or Jack. Be smarter than Claw here—don't offer the keys to the kingdom to anybody who seems mildly interested. Use what I've mentioned earlier and try to get involved in a mutual thing—hiking, bowling, getting piss-drunk, poker.

Stick your fingers in the mud long enough and you'll find a diamond.

BAKER'S DOZEN

"The ability to deal with people is as purchasable a commodity as sugar or coffee and I will pay more for that ability than for any other under the sun" - John D Rockefeller

How many men make up a Special Forces ODA? How many brains does it take to start a small business? How many outlaws does rustling a hundred head of cattle demand? How many people are actually in charge of or directing the World Economic Forum's globo-communist goal of Dekulakizing the middle class? Are you familiar with the maximum amount of braves you would want to take out a'raiding to not violate the most sacred of primitive tactics, aka the SKULKING WAY OF WAR?

The answer is baked into the cake; few. All of the examples I listed above take less than a dozen men. Twelve or less guys can run almost any outfit and I believe this is a tribal instinct—back in our hunter gatherer days, our hunting parties must have consisted of groups of such or smaller to maintain pace, divvy up the carcass of a kill, hold a small fort against the Enemy, etc. Twelve is a good goal but I'd be a damned fool if I said you could run an outfit of twelve on your own (that's why we have a hierarchy with at least two honchos beneath). Nevermind that, let's just outline why you want twelve and not more.

I've both taught martial arts and instructed groups at a number of community service events. What I've always noticed is that when you break the magic ten-twelve number in a crowd they immediately defocus and become disinterested in the 'whole' of the group unless they have a serious, vested interest in the project. Often when teaching karate I specified to my teacher that I preferred teaching the 9–12-year-olds as there were only about six or seven of them, versus the 5-8 year-olds who numbered twenty on a good Saturday. It wasn't age because on the days a flu was roaming the schools, I could keep their attention easy with half their number there. But with a full class it was harder than playing water polo with a watermelon covered in Crisco.

Focus on twelve for now—you'll be shocked how much effort and time it takes to amass more than ten people to gather, on their own volition, even when their life and bloodline depend on it.

It's not just attention-spans but intimacy of friendship; how many of your good friends do you keep tabs with on a weekly basis? How many can you call up on any given day and demand their free time to dedicate to a good bar crawl or game of cards on an evening? Now imagine that with twelve people who you've only met recently or haven't had the luxury of going to high school with. You're cultivating these friendships with the express intent of making allies, assets, and alliances that will outlast whatever hellfire awaits us in the years ahead—can you really juggle talking to a dozen plus guys every week and coordinate? I tip my hat to you if you can pull that off clean and solo while still maintaining employment, a marriage, and that frisbee golf membership or whatever fag hobby you have on the side.

Weekly you need to be communicating with these people (remember the Grandma Rule; anything sensitive/questionable/legally gray-area are to be kept on a notepad or confined to face-to-face) and with the express intent to—forgive me Father—*vibe with your gang*. Now Mr. Jack Donovan says that memes are bad—allow me to inform you that his only real job he's ever held down was as a go-go boy (fancy word for an urban gay prostitute), so essentially a walking hotdog bun ready to receive New York's finest sausages—so I'd say it's safe to discard this line of thinking. Memes are A) an effective, low-effort way to transmit big ideas with little words and B) usually dense with humor.

"IF YOU WANT TO GATHER HONEY, DON'T KICK OVER THE BEEHIVE"

Straight from the mouth of the prophet Carnegie; if you want people to like you/fuck you, breaking the ice and getting them to laugh at your messages is absolutely a must versus going for the throat with overly serious, intense communication. Broads and bimbos like serious guys who can joke around. Memes are universally charming. Suppose you picked extremely autistic, high-functioning retards who all belong to a European train enthusiast club; I question your judgement friend, but nevertheless you may have to be creative in your communication with the savants of high-speed magnet-powered public transportation. Just remember that laughter *is* the greatest medicine—it belongs next to the booze on the Getting Girls To Sleep With You shelf.

Don't overdo the dumb stuff for obvious reasons—months down the road if all you're sending are cartoons making fun of the most recent Entertainment Crisis™ and low-hanging fruit of politics—you're going to fertilize disinterest. Which is exactly why I'm going to suggest a novel concept that's never been explored in the history of social etiquette and fermenting friendships—hang onto your seatbelts folks.

Invite them to a BBQ. If you're not in America? Do a BBQ anyway because grilled/smoked meats are superior to pickled liver and spleen or whatever indigestible relics you eat over there and admit it, you think tailgaiting and

BBQs are the shit. Note that I didn't recommend to go eat out at any restaurant—that's intentional. You need to bleed cutting the onions for those burgers, burning fingers grilling, and demanding in the most Yiddish voice you can possess to be repaid for the relatively inexpensive foodstuffs (I'd recommend footing the bill here from time to time). One way to assume dominance in any crowd is to be the man with the cash.

Because what you're doing is re-enacting an ancient and primitive custom which is traced back to the wigwam and buckskin leggings of our savage ancestors; invite a potential threat into your tent (backyard) to enjoy the spoils of your harvest (brisket & drink) with the intent to negotiate alliances and displaying a show of charity (spending your time preparing the meal). The subliminal messaging by hosting a BBQ is showing your hands are empty of threats—invoking a powerful symbolism that cannot be overlooked.

Making these grill gatherings—monthly, quarterly, semi-annually—a consistent activity is a surefire way to win people to your side. Got a girlfriend, wife and a progeny of goblins? Drag them along. Boom! The other guy from your apartment complex has a wife and a kid of their own. Now they have a playmate and the wives have a potential friend—that's a knocking out who-knows how many birds with one piece of grilling charcoal. And don't overlook the loners; these are the guys you want to be integrating if they have any potential. Serve them all up.

"I HAVE NEVER MET A MAN SO GENEROUS NOR SO HOSPITABLE THAT HE WOULD NOT WELCOME REPAYMENT, NOR HAVE I MET A MAN SO GIVING THAT HE'D TURN DOWN A THING OFFERED IN RETURN"

The Wanderer's Havamal is right and rarely not; as a

host, your generosity and hospitality (if genuine) will be well-received. Gifts will be repaid with gifts. Reciprocity is a hell of a drug. I have never written a hand-written letter and had someone spit on it—this was a suggestion by a master of charisma I have adopted and cannot swear enough on the practice. Your perceived investment of time—especially that which is written and not typed—will be noticed by those who seek to bring into the fold.

Prehistoric man has not been living under a civilized, hyper-populated State with its anal-bead bureaucracies for the vast majority of our existence but as one of the following; a band, tribe, or chiefdom. These were the precursors to the very concept of ethnicity. Ignore the latter two—despite the fact so many misuse the word 'tribe', no it is not colloquial with a bowling league or your relatives—because neither are applicable to your posse. A tribe is a complex social and economical unit that is defined by the hundreds in a geographical region and a chiefdom doubly that and in the thousands—one day perhaps your ancestors will number as a tribe or even a chiefdom of tribes but delusions of grandeur can wait.

A band is defined by their mobility, their size, and their political autonomy; twenty to fifty men, can be divided into micro-bands, and ruled by a headsman or informal council. Hunter-gatherers were often divided into bands for obvious reasons; send four hunting parties for four mammoths versus one big party to bring down two at most. There's a social depth to band that cannot be overlooked—a band is tightly knit (better or for worse) as it is held together not by an economy or convoluted bureaucracy of laws but by the interlinking chains between each member. The laurels and the scars are shared by the members of that band, blame and pride run thick as blood, rarely will any challenge arise where it targets a mere individual.

Historically a band might have raided and scalped together but today they are members of a team—often working in concert for a corporation or commonly as athletes cooperating in a team sport. The headsman is easily replaceable with a team captain, the locker room the cliffs at twilight overlooking the enemy village, the 'playing strategy' the lines in the sand to represent the bird's eye of the battlefield. Why do you think when men watch sports they pick a team and call it 'theirs' with affection, LARPing as the headsman or one of the athletes? It's an instinctive kneejerk to associate yourself with a band—a survival mechanism that runs deep in your marrow—and as such, it's merely taken a new form in our commodified, modern society.

Picking your band—your team who may outlive you and rear your children—is an art of refinement. Whittling whom is worthy of keeping and who should be cut free and kicked to the curbside deserves a chapter in itself. Except I don't have to write a whole chapter—the Japanese already did when they invented the Bushido code. Full disclosure; I don't think the interpretation that the Shoguns during a period called 'The War Period of Decapitation and Annihilation' needed 'polite' and 'civil' warriors as nerds would have you believe—Japan devolved from a golden age into a decentralized, feudal state of warring chiefdoms who woke up and chose violence every day. The true meaning of Bushido—forged from that dark age—is not for everyday bugmen or individualists but powerful *tribal* people who seek glory, such as a small raiding party of sandal-wearing, manskirt-wearin Nipponese.

They are; Rectitude, Courage, Mercy, Politeness, Honesty, Loyalty and Restraint (by the way, if you recruited anybody who has all of these already, they probably graduated with a degree in International Communications at BYU and they're working for the CIA).

Samurai and the aspects of their holy, knightly virtues are disgustingly misunderstood today, fetishized purely for their aesthetics and by the 90's Ninja Moment. Let us not forget that the legendary blacksmiths who—with autistic reverence—forged their katanas after purifying the forge and wearing ceremonial robes to ensure that *even the blade as it was smelted and folded* was worthy of being held by an honor-bound warrior; its soul would be pure, not merely some item for brute and senseless homicide.

Bushido ain't no joke;

"MEN OF HIGH AND LOW STATUS, CLEVER MEN, AND ARTISTIC MEN ALL VIE TO EXHIBIT THEIR MERIT AS LOYAL SERVANTS, BUT BECOME LIMP AND CRAVEN WHEN IT COMES TO ACTUALLY SACRIFICING THEIR LIVES WHEN CALAMITY STRIKES. THIS IS INEXCUSABLE BEHAVIOR INDEED."

The inevitable conclusion and cornerstone of this sacred Japanese code is that all discipline should be in the service to death and death for cause; so too if you use this ideal, it can be the only evaluation whether you have 'masculinity' amongst your to-be gang. Need I remind you that a testosterone count is high amongst degenerates and losers even, beard-fetishists and those who have the affectations of men but none of the heart.

Grit sometimes likes to be invisible (it comes out with bushcraft, backpacking, and anything involving danger) but honesty and loyalty are not. Most people have not received training on deception or are world-class poker players so catching them lying or being a general shitweasel is usually quite easy. This may seem redundant to mention but a man who is willing to lie to you about a small thing or turncoat over a minor disagreement is worth ejecting from your gang without warning or reconciliation. What would they compromise to you if their stomach was growling, their last meal three days last? If they have kids would they sacrifice you to the blue helmets to feed them?

Liars and shitweasels all have a tell—something I've picked up over the years. A friend of mine I'll call Gaptooth—a Nordic skier and overall fun guy, loved to lie and made an art of obfuscating. His father abusive and his mother shrewd and stern, Gaptooth learned that telling a convincing story played a smokeshow for his devious drug-dealing and petty thievery (his mother knew because his father ended up becoming a homeless schizoid). Years went by of his ditching school, coming late to shifts at our local pool, and to the cops that he honed this talent to fabricate the most colorful of tales. Gaptooth inevitably found his destiny as a door-to-door salesman, pawning security systems. Hell of a merchant I'll tell you.

No matter how clever the story is or lie, merely tally how many stories they tell where they fail, do something mundane, or otherwise appear to be the loser—you will start to see a pattern! Gaptooth's became obvious to myself when I noted that in the span of a year he'd conned a casino in Vegas of some $20,000, detained by the mafia's thugs, told he was going to be tortured...all for him to find a way out the backdoor and escape with his skin. What a thrilling and convenient escape! Except I confirmed these untrue when speaking to his ex-girlfriend who laid bare the truth that he was drunk in Vegas, blamed another friend who got busted, and he was caught cheating blackjack to the sum of some $2000 or other.

Gaptooth was a bluffer and while I don't mind a man who can outfox a fox, you can't trust a slick with your life. Not saying you shouldn't recruit car salesman—you should if you want human-sharp fellas, which I cover later in Gambler Rules—but you walk a narrow rope when you bring in someone who may bring only absolution for their hubris.

The Civilized World and its ethics are currently smoldering in a dumpsterfire right now and those you're recruiting should be capable of stepping into that moral gray area—such is in love and war. Even while that is true and certain Anglo American niceties are going the way of the dinosaur (and disturbingly quickly) it is pertinent that said fellas are loyal and honest if nothing else—at least to you and the Mannerbund.

Weeding out liars, thieves, and complainers is nobody's idea of a fun job—but it's critical. A chain is only measured by its weakest link. Ban them, bar them, or suffer a gutpunch down the road.

Being the leader of a band of eleven calorie-annihilating men in their prime isn't all worrisome when you can order takeout for relatively cheap, get together and play a game of cards on a cool summer's eve in your comfortable, air-conditioned apartment. It is when you have to feed said eleven men (yourself included) when every time you sit down for cards you can hear gunshots within a quarter mile and every night may be your last, rationing every grain of rice, every piece of rabbit jerky.

Keeping one person well-fed enough to build muscle and keep their immune system at its peak is actually quite expensive. In our posh modern period we don't think of food in units of energy but in a scenario where readily-available meals are scarce and starvation is the norm—in the 2020's this is even becoming a reality with supply chains collapsing—every grain of rice is as valuable as a drop of gasoline. Recall that in the medieval period, labor was considered more invaluable than ore, given that feudalism and plagues and a thousand other tribulations lead to a constant depletion of able bodies.

Based off a diet of vegetables, fruit, dairy, and meat (forget grain for the moment), you're looking at more than an acre a person and daily work to sustain a 2500 calorie diet. Do you have that now? Do you have the manpower to both farm and fight completely, off the grid? The answer is very likely no and even if it's a yes, my guess is you're chuckling because you watched everybody and their sister who wanted to go off-grid with their cottagecore homestead with only a 'designer garden' has learned hard and fast how much of a soul-grinding life that is—and that's just growing squash and strawberries *for fun*. Fuckin forget sustaining a person.

The point being; the Industrial Food System, for how toxic and depressing it is, keeps this whole train of modernity going and your existence has it to thank. It's also failing. So putting on our Reality Glasses here, you need to consider that this team you're building you have a responsibility to feed when times are rough and it's on your head whether they pull a mutiny.

Why else do you think that guerillas are dependent on the local populace? For easy pussy? Cheap rent? Singing and dancing?

"THE GUERILLA MUST MOVE AMONGST THE PEOPLE AS THE FISH SWIM IN THE SEA."

Thanks Mao. Perfect timing to be talking about food and summon the Saint of Murdering Your Own Citizens by Starvation, ain't it? Nonetheless you must realize that in our future your Gang is eating one of three ways; farming, earning, or stealing. And since mass livestock are going to be one of the first casualties of the collapse—making ranchers very viable candidates for your Gang or allies, by the way—and you're going to need the sword over the plowshare, then earning or stealing it is. And unless you plan on making an enemy out the local populace and actually becoming a cattle-rustling outlaw, you should consider what Mao is saying.

(During the turn of the 19th-20th century, did you know that children made up almost 25% of the labor force on farms? That's a totally unrelated and extremely fun fact)

Now imagine you disagreed with me about my baker's dozen suggestion earlier and how stupid you might feel, considering you have to feed some thirty souls every day. Or fifty. While defending everything you hold dear *and* going on the offensive. Do you think that those goofy communist twinks and their pow-wow CHAZ/CHOP really had a chance feeding all those lunatics with their five-square foot plots of eggplant or whatever the hell they were trying to grow? Imagine what cities are going to look like in the future of this collapse when they try the same, ripping up random bits of sidewalk and planting Frankenstein squash seeds that turn sour from the buried asbestos from the toxic earth?

I offer you a bet of every cent I make on this book, in all future writings—hell let's throw in all my gold and poker chips too—that the latter half of the 21st century will be an eternal war of Hunger and who can stave it off. Effeminate urbanites will be gouging each other's eyes out for peas and scraps of bread let alone a full Angus cow. If you or I have learned nothing these last two years it's the wonderful discovery that the metaphorical sphincter that controls a steady, affordable stream of our ZOGslop (industrial food) to our grocery stores can be shut off on a hair of a whim—for no good reason at all and suddenly the price of ground beef can triple almost overnight.

No keeping even just a dozen men armed, fed, and away from each other's throats will be a full-time job indeed.

The fearsome Apache Indians—at their lowest and most pitiable, save maybe today in their obese, mobile-home state—were able to conduct guerilla warfare and keep their raid culture alive even while Uncle Sam corralled them on reservations. A bunch of teenage braves ghostriding the whip; skulking under the naked moon and the bleary eye of some Kentucky sentry to go raid the Tontos next door for that American firewater and maybe a few rounds with the chief's daughter. Now imagine that primitive squad if they had a mission to replace their hedonism; set a fire in the barracks of the US cavalry, steal some horses and loot the armory in the chaos? Turn those raids into attacking infrastructure like wells or foodstores of the occupying Americans, make the land surrounding the White Mountain a hostile, thorny moat of hell? I don't hate my own race but damn, what a sight that've been.

Two things a small band or primitive squad of twelve or less offer; stealth and speed. Wars overseas are being fought today in the hills of ancient Alexandria with drones filling the skies like arrows and guerillas riding dirt-bikes like nomadic horselords. Why?? Because everything today in the 21st century hinges on the *instantaneous collection of intelligence and how it can be deliberated on* (aka communicated via the net or radio). It is impossible to hide supply lines of trucks or compounds from a fleet of nigh-invisible eyes in the sky—cheap drones that can report back to some sweaty spook so they can airstrike or call it in. Now imagine how impossible that scenario is for McFatty in the drone trying to pin you and your posse down as you whip X-Pro 125cc's into a forest or the urban jungle, splitting twelve ways to rendezvous at a secret location.

Lawrence Keeley illustrates the following on our beloved and treasured savages;

"THE APACHES SURVIVED CIVILIZED MILITARY PRESSURE SURVIVED FOR ALMOST 300 YEARS AND WERE ONLY DEFEATED BY PRIMITIVE METHODS—LITERALLY BY OTHER APACHES WEARING U.S. ARMY UNIFORMS!"

Earlier he speaks of the context of the success of these literal turncoat Apaches as bands of men—contradicting the Army's previously unsuccessful attempts to subdue the Southwestern Scourge by means of wagon, calvary, and every other 'civilized' tactic of war. Spanish, Comanche, and American! The small, tight-knit, bands of Apaches could only be hunted down by their equivalents and the White Man because their mobility and stealth was turned against them. Their defiance and SKULKING WAY OF WAR was only possible because of their distinct, squad-sized outfits (whom were either related or intense friends) where other tribes had failed to resist or fight back, like their Navajo or Pueblo cousins. The White Man had to think tribally and against the grain of industrialized, macro-strategy to even have a chance at winning.

You don't have bigger brains in that bonehead of yours than the Apache had a gut instinct for sneaking and slitting throats. If He—who'd never seen anywhere that wasn't covered in red sand and cacti, nor read a book about war (or read a book at all)—had figured out that wielding dozens of small bands to fight with instead of larger ones would last him 300 years against overwhelming odds, firepower, and the logistic fist of the greatest nation to ever exist, I think you can trust the Apache enough to follow in his footsteps. Better yet; do you think that the oversocialized, moralist, shitlib urbanites who are already driving our civilization into the ground would be able to *adapt* to bands of decentralized, mobile guerillas better than the frontier-facing White Man did back then?

I cannot offer you a complete panoptic how-to guide on how to judge the vagabonds you've recruited into your posse. Or how to create some vague shadow-warrior gang. I never joined the military (like maybe I should have). Except unlike your average SEAL I actually know how to cement people together into sticky piles of camaraderie. Uncle Sam ain't always great at teaching people people skills, go figure. That's why I'll hire them eventually to guard my undisclosed-location mountain fortress.

I have dozens more stories of how to discern a friend from foe, how to pick out a bad apple, and what the qualities are of a man who you can rely on to watch your back in mildly dangerous/criminal situations. And they're all folly in face of experience—ahead I discuss the rigors and tests you can put up to see if they shake out to be Goon material or if they wash out and serve as a lesson. Other than that, it's on you to make that call chief.

Serious and intentional friend-forging, if you can call it that, is something that virtually no normie ever considers. Their friends are more like convenient acquaintances who like the same spandex superhero movie, junkfood joint, or played trading cards as kids in high school. They don't rely on these people for anything more than a justification to spend money on hobbies and a name to send out a wedding invitation to. Human friendship and bonding is instinctual but our modernization has lead these to be superficial and hollow links—ones that amount to nothing more than infrequent association and rarely intermarriage or anything lasting.

MOST HUMAN CATTLE TREAT KINSHIP AS A CONVENIENCE AND NEVER LEARN TO ENCIRCLE THEMSELVES WITH SKILLED INDIVIDUALS.

Creating a posse of a dozen or so men—ala this totally legally protected and inconspicuous 'Men's Club'—who are reliable, industrious, loyal, honest and all the other trading card stats for the purpose of survival in the 21st century is virtually unheard of. Naturally this optimistic cause in itself will create a gravitational pull for likeminds, saving you the exertion of selecting good eggs from bad. By selective (and secretive) advertising people will pick up on your—dare I say it—vibe and approach *you* because they've been thinking the same for months even years. Chances are if they take the initiative, they're bound to be driven and more reliable than anybody you have to shake down to come out to the hills with you on a weekend.

Now grab those dozen and let's get cracking.

TOO MANY INDIANS, NOT ENOUGH CHIEFS

"Friendship is necessary and ennobling; but impersonal despotism is destructive of all dignity and manly virtue." - Ragnar Redbeard

Agamemnon was a reprobate WOG! In every translation verbal and written of the Illiad is really just an instructive lesson on how not to be an unlikeable faggot-king. He got the golden spoon (crown) from his father, lost his cool constantly and never never ever learned how to *earn* his title. He was history's first trust-fund kid and his name will forever be worth less than the wormfood made from the Trojans that his men threw into the phalanx-woodchippper. Agamemnon was the worst kind of leader—a narcissist, the equivalent of a Bronze Age Theater Kid—taking credit for the laurels of noble Achilles. I'm not entirely convinced that Agamemnon wasn't Greek but actually a Yid who posed as an olive-pirate all so he could get some interest-free plunder. *Those* people rarely make officers or people who can command by charisma alone. Fucking greaseballs.

For generations the Illiad was repeated not in the written word but over a fire or in conversation by sailors and craftsmen and the common Greek—it was the mythos of a people. So when Agamemnon is depicted as a striver and wannabe, this is a folk tale and he is representing an archetype of a failed leader. Very few written histories ever account for their king or emperor's failures, labeling him as some reject! This is akin to modern day warehouse jockeys creating a story about a supervisor they had who was a hall monitor shithead and this story somehow makes its way to corporate, memorized and repeated for decades to come. Imagine you are so hated by your own men that your name summons derision even a thousand years after your rule.

Never be an Agamemnon.

When the sparks that led to the prairie fire of race riots that consumed the summer of 2020 (and coincidentally concepted this book), I was attending a wedding. The occasion was momentous—a union that was meant to be, each family overjoyed for the celebration, every person attended purposefully and not merely for the free food. Flowers were in full blossom in the gardens and field, live acoustic guitar filled the air, and the spirit of the event was entirely optimistic. I was only made aware about halfway through the wedding that not 25 miles away a police car had been overturned and torched by the local AntiFags in the capitol—all bussed in I might add—and thousands had taken to the streets demanding blood of whites and middle class alike. The entire wedding suddenly felt consumed by a shroud of darkness. Nearly every person that informed me of this news had a violent gleam in their eyes—that polite Anglo veneer had snapped. Under their breath or brazenly they chattered about grabbing rifles and hunting down these "black-bloc thugs" in the streets like mere pests.

Old ladies and lunkhead cousins I've never imagine to think to threaten another, let alone go engage in counter-guerilla violence, demanded of me what *my* plans were, to which I replied: "*Let's wait this thing out, keep your family safe, and keep your gun by your bedside. Don't go to the riots, whatever you do. They're looking for a fight. They'll get bailed out. You won't.*"

Like snow dumped into an early spring campfire, it cooled off their savagery. Yet an unmistakable resentment lingered in the air, their fury leaving an imprint on the conversations for the remainder of the event...and long after.

The thought occurred to me a year and some later; what if I had a plan, even shoddy? Would they follow me if I told them to pack their kit and head right towards the fire and brimstone? Could I wielded this (foolishly, I would never recommend anyone to go looking for a quick prison sentence) energy and manpower to defend what my pioneer ancestors slaved so hard to build?

Man is always governed by a chief. If I'm wrong, explain Gandhi, Jesus, and Hitler—INGRATE! Sooner rather than later a pecking order will be established in your goongang; you want to grasp the initiative in this endeavor. Many in your posse will assume it to be you to lead—a no-brainer if you are the one recruiting and forging these bonds (or reading this book) but that opportunity will be usurped if you are unable to hold onto this temporary authority. And then all hell breaks loose. Be a captain or step the fuck down.

In our era of bureaucracy and feminized authority, flexing confidently that you are 'head honcho' and the headsman of this band will gain some deference by the sheer attitude. You'd be surprised how far you'll get simply walking into a joint and declaring yourself King Boss. But scant few people these days have the balls to take the mantle (and responsibility) of total leadership, as opposed to the Hollywood trope that only the most vile leather-wearing fascist dictator will assume any control of a group. And yet men will still despise you if you assume authority anyway, as it is as instinctive to question your superiors. Damned if you do, damned if you don't!

Because man wants a chief. Dawn of time stuff. But he doesn't want one he can bash over the head with a stick easily. What staves off the mutiny? What keeps your head on your shoulders? Will your men draw your face with crayons on cardboard scraps in memory (like miniature Stalin portraits) after you got eviscerated by a homemade claymore? Or will they neglect to even recover your body and refer to you as their 'wannabe captain' after the failed raid? Goon hypotheticals!

Long answer; you need to earn their respect. Short answer; you still need to earn their respect. In the Rome-sacking legendary Germania did a chief sit on the golden seat because he cashed out his brownie points to buy the biggest winged helmet? I turn to Tacitus...

"WHEN THEY GO INTO BATTLE, IT IS A DISGRACE FOR THE CHIEF TO BE SURPASSED IN VALOR, A DISGRACE FOR HIS FOLLOWERS NOT TO EQUAL THE VALOR OF THE CHIEF. AND IT IS AN INFAMY AND A REPROACH FOR LIFE TO HAVE SURVIVED THE CHIEF, AND RETURNED FROM THE FIELD. TO DEFEND, TO PROTECT HIM, TO ASCRIBE ONE'S OWN BRAVE DEEDS TO HIS RENOWN, IS THE HEIGHT OF LOYALTY. THE CHIEF FIGHTS FOR VICTORY; HIS VASSALS FIGHT FOR THEIR CHIEF. IF THEIR NATIVE STATE SINKS INTO THE SLOTH OF PROLONGED PEACE AND REPOSE, MANY OF ITS NOBLE YOUTHS VOLUNTARILY SEEK THOSE TRIBES WHICH ARE WAGING SOME WAR, BOTH BECAUSE INACTION IS ODIOUS TO THEIR RACE, AND BECAUSE THEY WIN RENOWN MORE READILY IN THE MIDST OF PERIL, AND CANNOT MAINTAIN A NUMEROUS FOLLOWING EXCEPT BY VIOLENCE AND WAR."

Wax all you want with the honey of compliments and gifts and your ear, but your mannerbund will seek a man of action—not a charlatan, but also one that holds the reins. This isn't something you can fake or cheat with charisma and if you do, it won't last long. This is similarly why professors and professional thinkers do not lead bands of men—they lack in physical prowess and even scoff at the notion that a chief leads from ahead!

What did the Germans of first century understand? That displaying a *vigor for victory* is the aspect of a chief—one who is not is one who rests on his laurels and sits idly on a cushioned chair. AKA if you lead a band of barbarians, expect to be there front and center of the danger, because otherwise is to show you're not willing to flirt with death to gain glory. Your warband is very unlikely to be made of the same grit as those mustached Germans who turned Rome into their drive thru for whores and olive oil, but you can still understand the simple equation; more competent men = need a chief with bigger balls.

You've been done a great disservice by way of HR departments and the public education system; deluding you into thinking that meritocracy means 'whoever is the most qualified' gets the big feather headdress or golden crown. It ain't. If you're a student of my thug philosophy—or Nietzsche—you know life ain't fair and it's rarely the person most deserving of their title or stature who makes the cut, if ever. Man is a pack of dogs run by the meanest dog (note I didn't say biggest or fastest). He's hungry like the wolf and driven by his instincts. Leave your ideals of man being this virtuous, rule-following aspect of God at the door—pick it back up when you're en route to Heaven or Valhǫll.

Dogs aren't stupid by the way—they're not suicidal machines of carnage, even the least domesticated of them all. We don't give them enough credit for managing to stick to our side and ride the elevator of evolution to the point where we're at now—purse chihuahuas are pathetic for obvious reasons, but it is miraculous that such a slippery little rat of a thing has even gotten this far.

So if you respect that every one of your men will be governed by his impulses, his carnal desires, and his desire to survive it becomes incredibly simple to earn his respect in return; provide a means in which he can fulfill all of these. A kind of lord except instead of dispensing land or treasures, you're giving out black eyes and promises of conquest.

Except....how the hell can you offer that in the day of the syringe...in our domesticated modern day of fuzzy handcuffs...

In my early adult years I decided on an impulse to be a lifeguard. It wasn't a terribly easy position—we had no chairs, were forced to pace the deck for 4 hour shifts (many of which I took doubles, sometimes triples) and it was managed poorer than a skid row gas station. Besides the sunlight and the camaraderie amongst peers—many whom I still call and some number in my goongang—it was not a sexy job. But most importantly; the lifeguards and the pool were all managed by a woman.

We named her the Troll and by thunder she was one—body, mind, and soul. With a trunklike body and a face that looked like a potato carved by a toddler with a spork (not to mention a lazy eye) she was notorious not just amongst us 'guards but the parents and entire neighborhood. She was that goddamn ugly. Regularly Troll would get into brawls with parents over miniscule infractions—throwing the book at them over pool chair and beer-cooler law in a heartbeat, crossing the deck and yapping her jowls like some pigmy orc. She was a mean, brutish thing who was the enemy of almost every due-paying member, her notorious waddling around the concrete deck, sniffing the air for misbehavior. The Troll was the most aggressively uncharismatic person I have ever had the misfortune of meeting. And she was our supervisor.

I was 15 when I signed on, got my certification, and was dedicated to the job. For the three summers I worked there I aspired to one day be a 'head guard'—to wear the red shirt and be the tanned, cool guy who waded knee-deep in gash. The Troll had different plans. She singled me out on day numero uno, finding fault in every one of my behaviors, labeling me 'troublesome' and 'stubborn'—to be fair I was both. Later on I discovered she had an actual, legitimate fear of men that were tall and even remotely handsome—only because she was a revolting pig who never stood a chance to be ploughed by a man besides her effeminate egghead of a husband. The Troll's hostility with the male guards for being male got so violent in fact, that on her last year she declared that all entrants to the head guard program nullified and she would be accepting only females, barring one highly competent head guard—she was overheard by one of the maintenance guys, who relayed to us, that she told her coven of asskissers that "*girls are just better than boys at leading*" with a smirk. I still chuckle about how much crow she ate when the HOA bigdick fired her over such incalculable mismanagement.

One such case was where we had a blue-face—a kid who got dragged by the lazy river to the bottom and ended up in a medevac helicopter down to the ER. And where was the Troll when the kid got dragged out of the water? Panicking and trying to console the girl who pulled the would-be fatality out, neglecting her duty to call emergency services, advise her lifeguards to render aid, or generally do any of the things she's legally liable to. No she was too busy playing mommy to a literal retard who ended up getting the boot because she got 'PTSD' saving a kid's life and refused to go out on shift—shit you not, the Troll covered for her until our Bigdick manager over the entire HOA laid down the law. But who saved the kid's lives but the adolescents who took control of the situation while the Troll was nowhere to be found. A life might have been lost because of this Gen-X hall-monitor wanted to be a girlboss.

With every passing summer it became more and more obvious that the Troll was wet rag of a supervisor but most importantly she neglected even a basic level of commanding chiefdom. Her kneejerk reaction was always to deflect and point to her badge to say; "*um excuse me but who is in charge here?*" The result? Madness. The workplace became inundated with shenanigans to spite the Troll and get back at her cruelties, to name a few; sneaking our bikes in and throwing 'backies' into the pool, shitting into the hot tub and sticking the logs into the filters, covering the desks with hand sanitizer and lighting them on fire, lying that we 'heard lightning' to close down the pool early, and capturing roaches from the basement to stuff dozens in the girl's lockers (including Troll's).

There was one incident I'll never forget; the HOA had a vault of pancake mix and those godawful frosted cookies stashed for various holidays. On an evening shift all the lifeguards but myself—being on thin ice already—fashioned the cookies into frisbees and attempted to disc-golf them across the pool to hit each other. Naturally the pool became a red creamy bathtub. They were caught of course—the security cameras recorded everything including myself, not participating in the tomfuckery for once. One thing lead to another and soon I found myself in the office with the Troll, who pulled a public school teacher and accused me without proof; she assigned me to write a 1-page apology letter to her, the manager, and the ritzy HOA company for 'damaging property' (cleaning chemicals to keep the pool sanitized).

I told her to pound sand.

The Troll—all her stunted squat body quaking with giddy malice—marched me to the Bigdick's office, babbling about how I was about to get canned. She thought I was intimidated, totally incognizant of the fact I'd been charged with an ~~almost-felony~~ misdemeanor; a hit and run—losing all the money I'd made the summer before and going through court proceedings had seasoned me to the System.

I stood before Bigdick and said; "*howdy chief, I didn't do it and she's lying*."

A volcanic discharge of salt rained in that office—the Troll lost it completely. I'll never forget her face inflating like a balloon and turning four shades of hell, screaming that I'd be prosecuted for a cookie crime I didn't commit. All the while Bigdick sat calmly, nodding, and only asked the occasional question for clarification—he knew I wasn't on the security footage and asked me if I would stand by my position if he were to; I told him to go right ahead. The Troll had lost the plot, her incoherency was part-babble part-insult.

Because she wasn't just doubling down on her threats knowing I wasn't guilty—she was doubling down on her general disgust of me, to which landed her in the hot seat. All of her leadership evaporated that moment, her delegated power gone. Losing her cool in face of my stoic 'get fucked' attitude had proven to Bigdick I wasn't about to be made a scapegoat to slate her bloodlust. The guy actually apologized to me later on, even as far to tease a headguard position if I was to stay there—I wasn't because the goblinoid girlboss was still there that next summer.

The Troll taught me invaluable, innumerable lessons of leadership I carry with me still; nearly every day her cartoonish appearance and clownish number of fuck-ups an example of a 'not-to' guide for anyone, anywhere. But most importantly? When the chips were down her badge lost all meaning—her chiefdom was dissolved instantaneously when a crisis reared its ugly head. All respect and credibility to her title as 'supervisor' was gone—even from her trainee girlbosses—as one who could lead us. This is my warning if you want to play the chief;

NEVER LOSE YOUR COOL IN FACE OF DANGER AND NEVER FUCKING EVER BE A PUSSY.

Fight Club reaped a generation of men (Gen X) who said they were inspired to reject the gynocracy, start their own underground fight clubs, and retake their civilization. And what was sown? Middle-aged grifters who named Fight Club as their mentor, their bible, and then turned out to be losers faking wind in their sails to make quick cash—so-called Masculinity Coaches™ creating paid groups and 'mentorship' courses where they're the kingpin and you're the paypig with zero chance of a bar-cellar turned bare-knuckle boxing ring. Why didn't it? And why haven't these micro-celebrity 'Alpha Males' inspired any loyalty? The issue isn't a misinterpretation—it's the source.

The solution imbedded in Fight Club posed a simple task; provide a private and hidden space for men to brawl and reclaim that masculine virility—fighting and acting with their fists instead of with rules and regulations—and the plastic world would simply collapse in on itself. Isn't that divine and true? Nah partner. FC was actually missing something vital—something critical that only another author decades later fully delivered in his own bronze age collapse-themed book. And who inspired that writer but one from before—the father of the Ubermensch who says this;

"THE LEVELLING OF THE EUROPEAN MAN IS THE GREAT PROCESS WHICH CANNOT BE OBSTRUCTED; IT SHOULD EVEN BE ACCELERATED. THE NECESSITY OF CLEAVING GULFS, DISTANCE, ORDER OF RANK, IS THEREFORE IMPERATIVE — NOT THE NECESSITY OF RETARDING THIS PROCESS."

What does Fight Club miss that Nietzsche doesn't? That the act of underground brawling was merely a release—a fetishization of the act against the 'sin of violence' that the bureaucratic office-core era established *instead* of it being a trial to establish hierarchy as man naturally seeks a leader through such trials. A means to establish an order of rank. THIS is what is lacking from Fight Club; a call to underground clubs hidden from the eye of the globohomo, secret societies that will produce tribal thugs and gangs that employ this Ubermensch, not a fast track for individuals who've been freed from their monotonous life via a self-help jiu-jitsu course.

If Fight Club is the scapegoat for missing the mark, what's our bullseye for establishing a healthy pecking order in your posse? Longevity. A foothold in obtaining calories. Fight Club was reactionary—not unlike the dozens of micro-movements that have been spurned on by the Culture War. Nor did the gay writer ever consider that learning shepherding and animal husbandry would be more pertinent to the future!

Create a scenario where a martial/physical challenge is present, then offer a pathway to overcome the challenge with your hand of confident logistics present. Because—and not by sleight or trick—your Goons have to come to you for the itinerary and 'grand plan' but you're also taking care of the unsexy details, effectively being the bedrock of the whole operation. By backseating the fun, you're communicating; *I want this thing to go smoothly fellas.* This goes hand in hand with a concept I will attack later in the book I have learned among tycoons and sales champions, which is to always project a roadmap (even if you don't). Always be thinking two steps ahead.

I have a short anecdote for this; a good friend of mine Pony Boy went overseas to the jungle isles of southern Asia. He was the youngest of the group by almost a decade—the same age as Alexander the Great—his group being comprised of fuckboys and the female equivalent; social media 'influencers'. What rotten Chinese-souled rat people they were. As soon as their plane touched down, everything went tits up. The girls almost got kidnapped by taxi-minivan traffickers on day one, nobody had a schedule or itinerary other than Ms. Blockhead Narcissist who wanted to *"OHMYFUCKINGGOD we have to post at this skyscraper infinity pool today to advertise this our (yuppie brand) swimwearrrr"*, their passports got held for ransom by a scooter-dyke, and the fuckboys had a mental breakdown because of all the 'pressure' in tropical paradise. And then Pony Boy took charge when it was clear the guys several years his senior could control the situation as well as a fag could his well-loved sphincter.

"I REALLY JUST BECAME A CHILL DICTATOR."

Pony Boy told me reflecting on the entire situation. He would hold a meeting every morning where everyone would submit where they wanted to go for that day, how they were getting there, how long it would take them, and where the rendezvous was. Some of the dipshit influencers threw fits and one of them flat-out ignored him to drive through Sharia territory on her scooter, solo—later she complied when they ran into a troop transport full of hijab-draped women and Muslim dudes carrying machetes at the 7-11. The rest fell in line and they were able to hit all their points of interest, island-hop, go to ragers, cut down coconuts, and fight Muay Thai fighters for free drinks and had time to spare.

Point being, when he took charge of the situation he didn't say *"I'm in charge now"* or point to some invisible badge on his chest—he broke up their trip into manageable, small tasks with logistics and a little bit of surfer charm. He made their trip enjoyable and not chaotic pandemonium and his 'take charge kick ass' attitude came in handy when later they were almost marooned on islands, got deathly ill, and had a knife pulled on them.

What Ponyboy understood, if even accidentally; CREDENTIALISM CUCKERY IS A CANCER. Don't fall on your accolades or laurels—like age or 'muh experts'. Do you know what credentialism comes off as? Desperate.

And yeah, not everyone was happy with Pony Boy or his moves. One of the fuckboys' egos was pretty burnt up after getting relegated to playing a 30-year old grocery bagger and delivery boy. There was bad blood for the rest of the trip and it'd be a cold day in Hell before they'd invite Pony on another tropical excursion—not like he'd want to tag along anyway. It was *only* because of Pony Boy swingin his nuts around and doing some quick *CHIEFING* that he ever made it back on a plane stateside with a tan and that his whole crew of social-media idiots didn't in bodybags.

Being a CHILL DICTATOR is hands-down your best bet to running any kind of operation, period. Even if you lack that raw charisma. Like a surfer Mussolini. That's how we roll!

"THE AROUSING OF FAITH - WHETHER RELIGIOUS, POLITICAL, OR SOCIAL, WHETHER FAITH IN A WORK, IN A PERSON, OR AN IDEA - HAS ALWAYS

BEEN THE FUNCTION OF THE GREAT LEADERS OF CROWDS, AND IT IS ON THIS ACCOUNT THAT THEIR INFLUENCE IS ALWAYS VERY GREAT. OF ALL THE FORCES AT THE DISPOSAL OF HUMANITY, FAITH HAS ALWAYS BEEN ONE OF THE MOST TREMENDOUS, AND THE GOSPEL RIGHTLY ATTRIBUTES TO IT THE POWER OF MOVING MOUNTAINS. TO ENDOW A MAN WITH FAITH IS TO MULTIPLY HIS STRENGTH TENFOLD. THE GREAT EVENTS OF HISTORY HAVE BEEN BROUGHT ABOUT BY OBSCURE BELIEVERS, WHO HAVE HAD LITTLE BEYOND THEIR FAITH IN THEIR FAVOUR. IT IS NOT BY THE AID OF THE LEARNED OR OF PHILOSOPHERS, AND STILL LESS OF SCEPTICS, THAT HAVE BEEN BUILT UP THE GREAT RELIGIONS WHICH HAVE SWAYED THE WORLD, OR THE VAST EMPIRES WHICH HAVE SPREAD FROM ONE HEMISPHERE TO THE OTHER."

What must be discussed now on the subject of leading is that there are NO secular Great Leaders of history and if you are to stand any chance of inspiring you must be seen not as a transitory manager but as a preacher of apocalyptic sermons—not a TV evangelist preying on Meema and Peepaws cashflow from their reverse mortgage, but as a persona of The Chieftain who cloaks himself in spiritual language. The Boss. El Jefe. Big Kahuna. Without this almost religious fanaticism they have towards your charismatic 'image' (you must project this and constantly) you will inevitably fail.

I'm not telling anyone to go be a preacher ok. Nobody needs to go all goofy on me and wear those godawful Christian pantsuits. Look at how celebrities are worshipped and prostrated to today—tell me this is not religious fervor! There are no cheat codes to this since popularity is tied at the hip to having a devoted following and if I had that then I would not spend so much time on this book here and instead go off and become a celebrity. My only humble suggestion to garner such attention is to be eccentric in dress, mannerism, and speech to stand out but most importantly to FIXATE ON A PASSION OF YOUR FOLLOWERS AND EXCITE THEM ON IT.

As I stated earlier you cannot FORCE people to like you or your cause—even as a good storyteller. But look at social media today and influencers with passionate audiences! Like a goofy kid who drives various diesel-powered vehicles and dances the fine line of the law! He amassed a powerful gathering around him because he excites their fantasies of being daredevil stunt drivers and garage mechanics. His audience is vicariously living through him and his life!

Practice will make perfect but you must zero in on a passion or hobby or fantasy your followers want to enjoy so they INVEST IN YOU WITH ZEAL.

Start thinking about that future where you and your boys are staring at a deluge of refugees whose towns ran out of toilet paper or food, half of them urban looters (Kwan Bantoids) and your suburbs start looking like South Africa—when the families and children of your Goons are looking to *you* for consolation. Are you going to be a Troll or are you going to be a Pony Boy?

Plan a backpacking trip or mask up and plan an immersive LARP where you and your posse ~~walk and assimilate with the anarchists during their riot~~ stroll around an unsavory neighborhood. Detail everything, coordinate, communicate, and be ready to act on the fly. Layer this with a boxing ring and start dedicating serious time physically engaging with your Goons—they do need assurance you're not just a talker but a doer. Don't plan on becoming the next President of the Hell's Angels by doing this but you're not going to be eaten by the dogs either.

Above all dedicate yourself completely to being the Chief. This is how you earn your big talking stick.

SPECIALIZATION IS FOR THE BUGMAN

"A general is a specialist insofar as he has master his craft. Beyond that and outside the arbitrary pro and con, he keeps a third possibility intact and in reserve: his own substance. He knows more than what he embodies and teaches, has other skills along with the ones for which he is paid. He keeps all that to himself; it is his property. It is set aside for his leisure, his soliloquies, his nights. At a propitious moment, he will put it into action, tear off his mask." - Ernst Jünger

The 21st century will not be remembered for its colonization of the deepest reaches of space, its advancements in medicine and artificially distilling death, or its inhuman encroachment on the domain of the gods—cracking the code of 'what makes man *man*' by means of genetic fuckery. No the 21st century will be remembered as the Era of Failure and Hunger; we are all going to discover in a very rude way, that the very CRADLE of modern civilization is delicately perched on an oh-so fragile network of commodities zipping from one end of the globe to the next (thanks colonization) and that it isn't some natural force like El Nino but the brainchild of great men who knocked their skulls together and figured; "*hey if we can get bananas from Columbia to Chicago, we can feed that many more people to run our factories, who make us rich, so we can open more factories, etc etc*".

Rome was not glorious and its name chiseled into the annals of eternity because of how diverse its empire was; Rome was able to absorb multitudes of nationalities under its wing because it had the godlike ability to turn a stone-age tribal chiefdom into a settlement, afforded the amenities and staples of life, not to mention the shared protection of the legions. Rome was Daddy who built the home, brought the bacon home, and adopted your ass so long as you called him El Jefe. And when the empire of Rome fell, how did Rome fare; it corroded, rotted, and fell into a cancerous heap of bickering chiefdoms. Rome is remembered now by its bones.

Why is this pertinent to the topic?

Because what did Rome crumbling have in common with the Bronze Age collapse; more importantly *who* in common with these eras, survived these civic, societal apocalypses? Was it the masons or the public firefighters? The bankers? The farmers who toiled in the fields? Was it the fishermen who relaxmaxxed and ignored the total evisceration of his currency? Or was it the soldier who marched into yet another war against a neighbor by the Warlord of the Month?

None of them.

But the fief lords, tribes, and warriors; only they did. Why?

Specialization is great in theory. Why not have a vacuum-tech who only works on Japanese pufferfish-powered carpet cleaners? It creates a 'market' (funny how it means nothing besides carving a new slice out of the same economic pie) and everyone gets to enjoy the innumerable blessings of the capitalist deities! What could possibly be wrong about that? In the military having a specialization might be an ego-stroke but also provides some unique skills you might imagine, eh?

For starters the very word of specializing is rhetoric for 'limiting ones abilities to a finite field and set of — tasks' which is peachy if you're in a business of essentials where your services are *always* needed or marketable. Ever wonder why that the real economy is always revolving around the needs of housing and not what the current fad is? Dirt salesmen continue to have jobs despite being very un-specialized! Humans have the same needs we did ten, twenty, and ten thousand years ago; food, water, sex, maybe a cave to sleep in. Only the issue is the last century, the First World has outsourced its ability to do anything but specialize in the most useless and niche of fields—I *will* go full apeshit in any other occasion mentioning the favorite of eunuchs, ala 'service economy' but that's what it is; servicing the peasantry. Keeping the gravy flowing.

Special is a trick word a PR team invented to make you think that your button-pushing job is refined, elite or unique. This keeps middle-age midwits from eating a revolver when they realize their position as 'Assistant Manager' means they are a ring of the corporate digestion system—a literal sphincter designed to push email sludge along with boilerplate words that services a gluttonous stomach of existence—or economy in other words. Its especially devious when you consider that a child who has not mind-raped by the Public Education system can sustain themselves by grubby fingers and instinct even as they can't stand on their two feet. Their flesh is molded into the shape of a keyboard, a swivel chair, and computer mice.

Specialization is a nice word for enslavement.

Having your entire population specialize in business analytics and consultation—generations of cogs for a great usurious Machine—is great in the abstract value of Monopoly money and the magical GDP but long term it kicks you in the dick. Imagine all the cars today get wiped out by an EMP and suddenly you need 100k cars in production by tomorrow; how many micro-chip companies could be able or would be willing to retrofit their floors to start manufacturing quality, reliable automobiles? Could you have programmers start creating

Ford cars and trucks tomorrow, even on the governments dime? This isn't even a communist or fascist state—this is when disaster strikes a highly industrious, uber-industrial civilization and it has to stay alive.

Oh and the answer is none.

A first Gen. Mexican roofer who comes up north to leech off the Great American System can probably fix his own HVAC, works on his own Civic, knows how to properly farm asparagus. A second Gen aka El Housebroken Mexican can barely do his own laundry and works 25 hours a week writing popcorn articles for LA fashion magazine whining about White beauty standards as a 'LATINX' buttplug. This is not accidental. Being part of the Western, industrialized world absorbs you into this micro-segmented, hyper-atomized 'career' because it is the default state of machine-being; to proliferate as many possible people with as many standardized jobs, not so they are 'independent' but rather demanding the total obedience and integration of every participant like a gigantic centrifuge requiring hundreds of millions of specialized cogs to keep it moving—a more biological example would be a gigantic mushroom colony that requires more corpses to expand its fungal reaches.

Civilized Man born in the specialized role is afforded the path of least resistance—my proof of this is in food. With automation and social media delivery apps, you don't see an explosion of new or cutting-edge options but rather a GROWTH of existing fast food, obesity almost doubling, and the rise of lost art of a home-cooked meal. We have entire generations of pig humanoids who cannot and will not cook their own food—the bugman keyboard-jockey who snorts at the thought of cooking his own MealPaste because he's an enlightened professional who does his coding on the VR hellscape while a Chinese robot plunges a pleasure rod into his anus—a silicon sodomite.

This is the true end state of 'specialization'.

"THEY DEMONSTRATE HOW MOTIVES OF BUREAUCRACY ARE DIRECTLY OPPOSED TO THE NEED FOR ADAPTING TO CHANGE. ADAPTABILITY IS A PRIME REQUIREMENT FOR LIFE TO SURVIVE."

Frank Herbert (**DUNE**) says. No further comment needed.

You are your weakest link; the Achilles tendon can render the most athletic specimen into mincemeat for the rats. Tribes and groups are no different.

There is a reason that in the Boy Scouts, you put the fat kid in the front; it is not to punish the 14-year-old Aryan future supersoldiers who can ruck 65lb over mountains but to teach the fat kid that he is the anchor that drags their party down. It is humiliating on purpose. An elk herd is not troubled by abandoning their weak elderly or even young to the wolves—is this immoral? Imagine you are being hunted by drones in the neo-suburbian favelas and your 'fat kid' consistently plays music from his Bluetooth to let everyone know where he is; will you tolerate him compromising your hideout, your Goon compound? Or do you shoot out his ankles and leave him for the mindless horde of scavengers? Do you leave him like the elk do their weak?

Recruiting was the easiest step—this difficult one is to weed out those who do not belong, who are not dedicated to a path of pain, chance freedom by criminality, to accept a coyote life.

The most important part of organization is not what you do but who you do it with.

Intoxicated by the dream of the Wild, I and two of my gang decided to undertake a true mountain man trek; the goat trip. A no-holds-barred expedition delving over a hundred miles across high tundra; across country along the tops of prehistoric mountains that demanded a brutal regiment of 20 miles a day, we would summit passes of the horned and white-coated goats, mountain lions, and tiny alpine voles totally exposed to an unrelenting sun and the squalls of Thor or some other vengeful entity who claim the realms of the alpine. It was a harsh and essential lesson on depending on each other for survival—few if any other men I know have gone through such a thing, even on a deployment to the desert or voyage into godforsaken jungle.

Traveling such long distances we knew would test our physical endurance—even as myself, having spent the months prior preparing by smaller 30-mile trips. My pair of companions were both former military since I don't trek with retards or the incompetent; Compass who was no stranger to the trail itself having attempted it once already, halted by wildfire and being sharp in outdoorsmanship and Corn; a denim-wearing fiend who was cursed into being born into the modern era and God owes him a favor for not kicking him down earlier to be a mountain man. All of us athletes ate 4500 calories a day and still lost 10-15 apiece. We had 5 days to complete our task.

How we were weathered.

The alpine sun scorched us like little melons and turned us into fruit leather. Our packs had to be under 40lbs and still they caused us anguish, blisters, and raw skin. Every injury swallowed, wound to our prides stuck like thorns, and the abuse of 100 miles was like salt into raw flesh.

When you undertake such a primitive pilgrimage, you are like a lost dog finding your way back into your primal past. It dawns on you on the third day of being around only two other humans, a hundred miles away from anything resembling a 'city' and that you are traversing a naked wildernesses that has only seen man in numbers greater than a dozen a year during the last Ice Age that you are truly isolated. Life here revolves around a hunger and animated spirit of regeneration and reincarnation between petrified stumps and vast taigas trapped in hump-like mountains who predate our species' existence. Here there is no support network, nothing that resembles anything remotely civilized. Every tool, every need you must bring with you—including your will not just to exist in a place that psychologically thrashes you one moment, then induces your senses of wonder not a breath later.

It is heretical to divulge every moment of the 100-miler; what I can say is that less than halfway into our journey I fucked up bigtime. In my idiocy I didn't check the liners in my 'runners, which were flatter than your prom date's chest. Combine that with aggressive cleats and most of the trail being moraines left over from glacial accumulation—in layman's terms, a never-ending highway of rocks that pulverizes your footpads—I was putting enormous strain on my feet. On our third pass and deep in mountain goat territory my left foot cracked under pressure—a very minor fracture but one that wasn't exactly dandy considering medical assistance was more than 50 miles in any direction, by foot. My companions were charitable and showed no signs of frustration as I hobbled down the steep decline for the remaining 12 miles of that day.

Foolishly I thought I could sleep it off and by morning it felt as though goblins had stolen into our camp attacked my foot with meat tenderizers. Leaning on my trekking poles I set off on that smoky red sun morning—it was so painful I was forced to stop every mile and elevate. Pain became me and I it. I rubbed the skin off my palms from gripping the cork handles of my poles which was a more bearable pain. It was all I had in my power to maintain my companion's pace, who tolerated my hobbling state (I was here on referred to as Pegleg for the remainder of the journey). Only when we ascended the largest mountain and pass of our journey—the Crown of the peaks—that we had the conversation I'd been dreading.

"Do you need to dip out? Bail? Look chief if you need to get out we get it. But then you need to take the next path," they said to me.

Proceeding over that spine that rose to straddle tarns and low scrub on our journey to the Crown I had a serious moment of soul-searching; endure and become a masochist or trade the next 50 miles for 10 to dip and become the second-biggest pussy God has ever kicked through the front door. My buddies would understand but I'd never live that down. So you can guess what my answer was as we ascended a brutal ladder of debris fields and made coffee at 13k; even if I suffered a broken foot, this trail was mine. I was gonna ride it harder than the first girl who opened her legs to me.

Fate struck at the most bizarre moment. As I uttered my decision, Compass got an alert after receiving less than 30 seconds of service; a freak snowstorm was to blanket the area 2 days from that night. It took minutes for us to comprehend how divinely fucked we'd been. When you have about a month and a half window to take your hyperlite gear on a 100 miler in that country, you're not counting on 2' of pure powder in fucking August. But it did. It was an all-time record. Some kind of luck huh?

In our descent to the adjoining valley the decision weighed heavily on Compass—we delegated to him to make the final call as it was him chomping at the bit, being cockblocked the first go-around. His struggle played out in his locked jaw and chewing his lip. Back and forth we tried to out-reason, out-rationalize the storm.

We could beat it in two days. We could pick up the pace and turn 20 miles a day into 25—a deathmarch but we were willing. We stewed over what gear or foodstuffs we could dump. We looked over our GPS for shortcuts. We thought of every possible contingency and loophole so we could make this trail our bitch, all 100 miles. Beneath a waterfall and shit-you-not rainbows, we could see the sign that veered off to the right; Castle, the last possible exit before the trail turned south to hump over our final passes.

Picture the most picturesque valley you can think of—a vision straight out of Tolkien's imagination, add a balmy 85 degrees and not a cloud to mar the sky. The weather can turn on a time up there but we had 2 days—we had no reason fathomable to the ways of our civic religion of Science that would suggest we should take a right hand to Castle and leave glory behind. None. If we had been bugmen who stare at the pixels on our screens, we'd have sworn by the satellite people and TRUSTED THE SCIENCE (the forecast that the storm was going to hit us on Thorsday) we would have walked headlong into annihilation, marshalled by the metaphysical Fate.

How many moments do you think people have had this kind of trust put into them; to trust Man and his Technical Gadgets or to trust in the acids in his gut which are churned by the Norns? This was ours.

Compass—my pagan brother—turned to us and said he thought that the gods were telling him something; a daydream since our ascent kept repeating of a horrific, life-ending vision that would occur if we did not bail and take Castle Pass. They had hammered it into his skull every time he tried to dismiss it. What I have not told you yet is that my mother had the same dream two weeks before—me trudging through deep snow to the knees, lips frozen blue, dying a Nord's death.

Try to place yourself in his boots; you attempted this journey the summer previously only to be thwarted by a freak forest fire not 15 miles down the way. You've financed this trip, sacrificed life and limb to get here, and now you get a dream that tells you to abandon the trail—AGAIN!

"Dreams are just juices of the subconscious powered by our meat skeleton. There are no oracles" a nasally Redditor sneers somewhere, suffocating on his own spit—hopefully to die. This is the subhuman knuckledragger who would have trusted the satellite weather and wouldn't go outside if Tech App warned him not to.

I will say this; two ravens circled above us on that pass and watched us carefully to weigh our souls. The choice we made was not a light one.

Compass made the final call. Here's what ensued; we hitched our packs and hit the trail running; not but 15 minutes later, a hailstorm pelted us non-stop; we ascended the pass, black clouds stole into the valley with lightning speed, billowing and covering the peaks with walls of moisture; and as the storm nipped our heels, we regretted nothing of our decision. By the time we came down into the mountain mere the rain sheets were slashing, thunder pounding, and we made a quick shelter with moments to spare. 17 hours of relentless downpour followed like I've never seen in that range, mountains gushed open and flooded the lakes tenfold—have you ever seen the high alpine rendered into swamp? You wake up in a frozen puddle. Corn had the early stages of hypothermia—giving us less than 10 minutes to pack our shit, totally soaked, and get down to escape the wrath of the gods. We burned rubber. And made it still with smiles on our faces despite not owning a single dry thing by the time we got to the bottom.

"Life is miserable when you're cold or wet; you better

be a masochist if you're both."

On our exfil from the mountains a bull moose—I believe must have been a god or a messenger of some skinwalker-tribe, wearing the skin of a beast—escorted us to the bottom, dancing amongst the birch and flooded wetlands. If you've never seen a ton and a half of muscle and antler leaping and weaving through trees like a fish deftly moves through coral, you have been denied a meaningful existence. Even to recall it now seemed a dream.

Dream is a profane, terrestrial word to me after this journey. You now should understand why.

This mountain-goat trek resembled something far less horrific or destructive than what many fantasize as the 'Great Collapse' but did serve to instruct the heavy lesson on the futility of individualism; that even with a nomad team made of survivalists and killers decked out to the teeth with the latest and greatest kit were unprepared for a few flakes of snow and barely capable of 100 miles. Imagine weeks in the wild. Imagine months. You may not reproduce the same bushcrafting but you get my point. Man is utterly crucified by his relationship to his toys, his tech and creature comforts—it isn't farce to fantasize that he could hack it on his own in the event of an apocryphal event, even a natural disaster such as Hurricane Katrina. It is fetishizing an ideal of what modern Man is capable of.

To be more introspective Man in many ways is threatened today by the prospect of 'losing it all'—his hyper-financed and leveraged lifestyle that has become his identity. Cushioning yourself with credit only serves to cripple you for tomorrow.

Never forget that you are a beast with a soul and you can control how weak or strong you will be—you are not a button-pushing monkey unless you let yourself be.

"WORK" WAS A CURSE, AS IN THE BIBLICAL STORY OF THE GARDEN OF EDEN. AND NOW, SINCE THE EIGHTEENTH CENTURY, INNUMERABLE "HANDS" WORK AT THINGS OF WHICH THE REAL ROLE IN LIFE (EVEN AS AFFECTING THEMSELVES) IS ENTIRELY UNKNOWN TO THEM AND IN THE CREATION OF WHICH, THEREFORE, THEY HAVE INWARDLY NO SHARE. A SPIRITUAL BARRENNESS SETS IN AND SPREADS, A CHILLING UNIFORMITY WITHOUT HEIGHT OR DEPTH. AND BITTERNESS AWAKES AGAINST THE LIFE VOUCHSAFED TO THE GIFTED ONES, THE BORN CREATORS. MEN WILL NO LONGER SEE, NOR UNDERSTAND, THAT LEADERS' WORK IS THE HARDER WORK, AND THAT THEIR OWN LIFE DEPENDS ON ITS SUCCESS; THEY MERELY SENSE THAT THIS WORK IS MAKING ITS DOERS HAPPY, TUNING AND ENRICHING THE SOUL, AND THAT IS WHY THEY HATE THEM."

You may not now afford to ignore but never for once believe that this hyper-commodified 'labor' is somehow a natural system of value that represents anything tangible or accessible to the common man. They have dressed down what was once called slavery and rebranded it with the skin of feelgood corporate jargon like 'content' or 'stuff that does stuff that makes stuff be stuff' which is all boilerplate nonsense to keep your fingers grinding down to bone and keep your neck bent to never lift and gaze into the horizon. As Spengler says above, the very concept of work or labor is a debt—it is a spiritual gulag and a raping of the soul.

A true Goon—a hunter who sleeps in a cave and fucks as he wishes does not *labor* like some pleb. He takes. He lounges. He savages his environment. He would never once consider the civilized man's chains of trading his body for minute luxuries except only as a tool to further his own conquering; i.e. money, power, or dirt. He is the monolith of nature's specimen of pure warfare.

If we believe in the premise our First World is collapsing—a fact indisputable by the law of all civilizations—then it is *undeniable* that the first aspect of modern life to be eliminated will be the blocks of free time that only the middle and upper classes enjoy now. Vacations will be annihilated. Break periods will be mandatory thirty minutes maximum. The World Government will only allow you to leave your Work Cage to get your sterilization shots and hormone blockers. And this will continue in this pattern even as the trains stop coming and the power stations are immolating. It will be a very dark time to be a low-caste depth groveler...partner.

Imagine you, future mighty Goon chieftain, can secure not only a piece of arable land or an office block where you can employ fellow Goons but amass the loyalty and prestige among your them same as any warlord or mafia capo by offering them the freedom to wander or lounge—if anything by not have to slave every waking moment of their day for meal-tickets or barter-scraps. An ounce of loyal blood is worth tenfold what mercenary diligence gold can buy. It isn't even about the reward you receive but the deep knowledge that you spared your comrades from an automated favela future with manufactured hyper-inflation, ushering in an age of human chattel of unparalleled cruelty in the name of profit.

In antiquity LABOR was known as death. Working with your hands meant you would die a young and painful death. Why do you think that in India they have slaved to send their sons over to America to become soft-handed tech nerds or doctors? The quality of a streetshitter life is less than a gnat—this same densely-populated gutter civilization of toil is exactly what the Overlords of our System want YOU to inherit. Why else do they feed you cheap cattle-feed and treat you like a herd?

Obtaining the ability to employ yourself or to work less and less for 'The Man' and still build wealth is an endeavor now that might just seem more idyllic or 'upper class' but I swear to you, on all the Gila bones under rock and ancient sunlight, that one day you will NOT ONLY see the toiling hordes debasing themselves just for a lab-grown rat filet—they will beg and slobber at the mouth to live as drug-addicted SLAVES.

And you will mutter under your breath:

"Claw you were goddamned right!"

GAMBLER RULES

"They call me a drifter, they say I'm no good
I'll never amount to a thing.
Well I may be a drifter and I may be no good
There's joy in this song that I sing"
~ Marty Robbins

Poker is to the keen Goon what the Bible is to the penitent or the blueprint is to an architect; a guide on not merely navigating the treacherous waters of human interaction but harvesting it for its flesh and teeth.

You'll never learn this at business school or leadership counseling or whatever grift is trying to sell commodified 'salesmanship' aka the watered- down art of manipulation. In Ancient Rome this would have been also called statesmanship because the cruel and intelligent creates empires from this. Fuck Freud and his 'Jewish mind' masturbation—aka the lower-than-a-snake's-belly science of psychology, which you should erase from your brain. If you want to truly learn the human psyche, sit down at a $5 Hold Em table and observe. Savant Science.

I learned this not long ago.

Instead of going to the gilded establishment aka College, otherwise known as the factory of mud-hut vagina communism on how to become a button-mashing email-professional, I learned white collar crime. No classes but a tutelage by a hustler who taught me how to clean commercial fish, earn the respect of a crew, run a business like a mafia, emotionally blackmail clientele, hustle cash but most importantly play cards. Oh you played some Blackjack with your college fraternity? Very cool Russell, also nice pink thong around your ankles!

Skirting around the low deserts of the Southwest without a job and $2000 to my name, I met my match; a dirt-slinging silvertongued sonofabitch. If he'd been born 150 years prior he'd been that archetypal Gambler who'd be dodging towns to avoid vengeful losers and their pistolas (maybe Maverick like the Mel Gibson movie) and that's what I call him. His mentorship was a trial by fire—priceless and mean and cunning and perhaps shouldn't be recorded by any human hands for fear of his retribution. But I am compelled by trickster forces and the gods of vice who tell me my readership *need* to understand these rules.

The Gambler didn't play for money. He played for the thrill because man to him was a puppet. This was a man who spent years in the lightless northern coasts fishing for crab, throwing his body into the cruel icy gauntlet of Fate for fun. And the money that comes with king crab. He was a pirate and a shyster who was only impressed with me enough to take me on because I had proven to him that I *understood* that people are wet machines. A sidenote but any true mentorship is like this; it *cannot* be bought. Same reason why going to school to 'learn' is an exercise in futility. Public school teachers are scolds by heart and the type of girl who has a desire to be an educator only because they want to remake future men out of spite of being underfucked if not at all.

A true craftsman refuses divulging their expertise to just anybody but someone worthy of that caliber and impressing upon them their total character which is why mentorship cannot be replicated for The Masses.

My education was that between gigs we'd sit at bars and psychoanalyze everyone in the room. Mexicans who swaggered around like bull dogs; they're the kind who bet without thinking. Old Asians acting neutral and reserved; they play close to the chest no matter how much is at stake. Retirees jollily downing hurricanes; bored and lonely guys who throw money at a table just to feel like they have friends. Every person has their read. We drowned in mannerisms and tics and juiced every detail from strangers with autistic fervor and they were none the wiser. I learned everything from him about poker with a whiskey sour in hand—rarely when I was actually holding a hand.

Novices will tell you everything to poker is about knowing the best hands or waiting on the river for that perfect flush so they can SoyFace like an excited downie getting his first handjob on the short bus—slapping his hand on the table and screeching in victory. This is the same kind of imbecile who will get rolled and taken for everything they have next game. Masters will not even look at their cards half the time. Some nerd will claim that some gigabrain that's foolish because if you can do all the cuck-ulations in your head you could figure out probability—while chances aren't to be pissed on, no nerd will ever be a Doyle. Even a Harvard Mathematician who picks up the game has to hide behind their autism or learn people-isms to bluff. And they get beat on bluffs all day because they don't got a drop of Alligator Blood in their veins.

Because *betting* is the real game of poker.

It is psychologically scalping people at a table who think they are hot shit by merely throwing money at them and scaring them into losing their shirt. This same Master poker player like Gambler will beat a table 9 times out of 10. He might not win the whole pot because he doesn't need to. He just needs to make the big stack fold *one time* to assert dominance and establish his superiority. It's about turning people inside out by reading them and ripping off their ballsack and turning it into a purse in front of everybody—especially if it's some Border Bandit Mexcrement who only wins because everyone else is too pussy to bet against him.

Projecting power and strength so that you *become* that projection is gambling, baby. Which is why you never come in by the skin of your teeth—throw cash like you *don't* care about it but don't throw your money at just anybody and go broke. Divorce yourself from attachment but calculate coldly who you want to carve up first. And if you can't afford to burn that $500? Walk the fuck away. Now you are realizing the parallels. The way people act at the table when you project power? They act the same way at the bars, in the wilderness, and especially in power.

You thought this wasn't still about leadership and Gooning?

Hold-em is just a mirror of human carnality and you should write down its every sacred code as the goddamned commandments.

"THE DIFFERENCE BETWEEN PLAYING GOOD POKER AND PLAYING GOOD BLACKJACK IS AS VAST AS THE DIFFERENCE BETWEEN SQUAD TACTICS AND GRAND STRATEGY IN WARFARE. YOU CAN BEAT A BLACKJACK GAME BY KNOWING EXACTLY WHAT TO DO IN EVERY SITUATION…AND DOING IT. THAT'S TACTICS. BUT IN POKER YOU MAY FACE AN IDENTICAL SITUATION AGAINST THE SAME OPPONENT, HANDLE IT TWO DIFFERENT WAYS, AND BE RIGHT BOTH TIMES. THAT'S STRATEGY."

Doyle Brunson is *the* man. Another book you should pillage is the Super System by the Godfather of Poker and Legendary Cardsharp. It is a goldmine of exploiting behavior, learning social cues, and the shortest literary trail to becoming a master of manipulation I've ever seen. You know the Communications Majors who make it into the 3-letter agencies never read this by the way—another edge you'll have that they don't.

So back to the Meatspace.

Your organization juices are flowing. Your Goongang is underway or already established. So why delve into game-psychology and Poker so heavy? All fair questions.

Because we don't live in a fair or holy world but a world of shadows and lies. A man's word is worth less than spit today which should be the very opposite, when it is so inexpensive to be honorable. You're being cheated daily. None of this is new information to you...I hope. I said "*...always fight fucking dirty...*" in my last book I believe.

Being the ringleader or being some kind of headsman will only paint a bigger target on your back—you'll be taken advantage of, stolen from, harassed and threatened for the privilege. King's burden. Poker directly translates to business as it does to leadership because every ante or call in the Meatspace could mean life or death. You're gambling with the lives of your Goons going down this path. And you should *never* play if you don't know whether your hand is worth shit or not.

Your Mannerbund will face thousands of possible scenarios, be it building networks of sovereign farmers and workers to trade, competing with cartels or rival gangs in the area, and brushing up against the actual law and their thugs. And you're a fucking moron if you aren't trying to calculate the odds of survival or trying to read the situation to try to pin the tail on your donkey—you're also doing your Goons a disservice by not pocketing every potential hand—i.e. the wisdoms to know every tell and bluff you encounter—you can because your ability to negotiate, spy, swindle, and chum it up on *their* behalf is everything.

"GAMBLING UNDERMINES THE MORAL FIBER OF SOCIETY."

Says Gordon B Hinkley, former Mormon prophet. And he's dead wrong. Even a chimp would assume the man is either suffering from an extra chromosome or doesn't understand that LIFE itself is a gamble. I don't bring up the dirty laundry of this quote merely to drag my former faith but because there is some wisdom to the idea that *all* one needs to do to unravel this so-called *"Ummmmm Excuse me but What About Our Moral Fabric of our Society?"* is to offer some low stakes in ones favor for even a humble reward to reveal the common weakness in your fellow man? Thanks for pointing that out Mr. Hinkley, Latter-Day Sucker!

Everyone has their price. Even for the so-called saints and martyrs of our current day who get their marching orders from Televangelists they all have to eat, sleep, and stay dry—more importantly what is the dealbreaking reward? Do not forget that during Hurricane Katrina the church-goers had extensive and concrete supply networks that sheltered each other first before lending a hand to the anarchy around them. They were unto islands among the apocalyptic tide, literally and metaphorically. Do you think that they would have appeared so noble and charitable if they were lone and without pre-established communications or supplies stashed well in advance? Did you also know that during Hurricane Katrina there were cops and men of the moral cloth who went bandit and settled old scores during the pandemonium—taking the law into their own hands and head-canoeing whoever they pleased, Doc Holladay style.

Everyone has a price is just a polite way of saying everyone has their g-spot, their Achilles heel, their vice. Most people won't turn their nose up at cash. Don't forget that little tip by the way. A credit card is a plastic card representing an abstract number on an internet database with no actual hard assets or gold—having a wad of cash in hand will never not project your power while softening your mark's knees—be them a Goon or a target. This is why no matter how 'digital' our society ever becomes that you will always have Egyptian cotton, leopard print, gold cufflinks etc.

(Nothing in this book is advice of course, you already knew this. It's pure comedy and satirical jest!)

Which is why no one in their right minds would ever use this sub-section to consider anything as egregious as bribing a local bureaucrats with a free steak dinner to make a greasy friend (never ever say this in writing or admit to anything other than just being a grateful person, as anything that isn't recorded and verbal cannot hold up in a court of law) or to offer the stakes of an investment (cash is inexplicably what the bad guys like to use apparently) like land or flipping a property or invisible shares in your company, etc. No you definitely do not want to ever slip anyone cash or non-traceable tender (like favors from a restaurant you handsomely over-tip every time you visit because you have a mafia-relationship with the manager) because that's unethical, even illegal! Only some kind of unethical Goon would think about whether it would take Benjamins or Lincolns to sway someone to look the other way or aid them!

It's not as if every cardsharp and poker machismo from the last century has confirmed with hard data and Poker guides that the majority of players (your everyday Joe Shmoe) are 'fun players' and will throw cash at a table (take a bribe, commit petty crimes, do some hooligan shit) because they want to see a good game through. It's *definitely* not that the thrill of gambling drums a man's heart and elevates his pulse...no these are merely coincidences that Vegas is still around and everyone wants to go there!

After all the very wise Mormon Prophet said that the

moral fabric of our society is intact without a physical table or slot machine anyhow...

A rarely discussed fact of the chaotic era of the Wild West buried by the zealous feet of the Reformers and the Manifest Destiny fantasy is that a staggering number of sheriffs, deputies, and lawmen would hop state lines to commit all kinds of criminality, rustling cattle, plundering trains, even murder....

That 'good guys' go bad for the sport of it.

Roach, a friend with a sharp mind when it comes to criminal history says;

"BOTH OUTLAW AND LAWMAN SELECTS FOR THE SAME SET OF SKILLS ON DIFFERENT SIDES OF THE CAPITAL L LAW; THEY ARE TWO SIDES OF THE SAME COIN."

There is more to the meta. I think that the steeper stakes and the ever-narrowing risk of being caught with the birth of the lawman drove many a 19th century Goon to reconsider his prospects; ala the juicier bounties and redemption the State offered that an outlaw turncoat. There are valid theories that even the infamous Butch Cassidy and Sundance Kid were informants or even working for the Pinkertons as their whereabouts and activities were always publicized while comparatively the James gang or other notorious bands had a sliver of such dirt on them—besides spiteful lovers or bad luck, this does raise the brows.

Roach says more in his 'Bank Robber Theory'; when comparing the nigh-inhuman aptitudes of your modern special forces and an American highwayman you start to see the same patterns; intellect, ruthlessness, disagreeableness, creativity, and suicidal ambition. They are the same person working for opposing sides—only that the System now has creative means of disarming this barbarian by lucrative paychecks, American-Sniper type propaganda, and of course a surveillance apparatus to carefully watch their most elite attack dogs.

Part of this propaganda—you may have even guzzled by accident—is that during the Vietnam War a 'new' breed of soldier was made; the brush-tiger commando. Instead of the redneck infantryman drafted to guard depots or catch ambushes you had an anti-guerilla who thought like a guerilla, conducting supply interdictions, working behind enemy lines and operating independently with no support network! WRONG! This was just a legal bandit given high-speed tools and given a license to pillage! He would have fit into any posse 100 years earlier. I think Roach is on the money, also considering that just buying these people at bargain-rates (i.e. the price of a soul) was not a done-deal for life. MAGV-SOG men were extremely dangerous and unpredictable; they needed to be '*handled*' when they came stateside which conveniently parallels the timestamp where the modern American security state really took off...sure makes you wonder eh....?

A micro-history lesson but an important one; dangerous men are a liability to any system of governance in the same way a highly-aggressive and competent player is to the House...long-term. A gunslinger is still a gunslinger. And if the so-called 'Sheepdog' class has already been bought with a contract and a stack of cash—even for Uncle Sam—then that means that they can be bought. Period. They have a price.

Who do you *know* can't be bought? A rhetorical question.

"PLAY LOOSE IN A TIGHT GAME AND PLAY TIGHT IN A LOOSE GAME."

Commands Brunson. Kingly advice. At all times and especially when you want the upper hand you need to be unreadable as you can. A fool will assume this just means bluffing—otherwise known as a cheap lie which is *not* what I am saying. People expect bluffs and for you to put up walls whereas they never expect you to play the sucker. Ask yourself what's more unnerving? If I acted real keen my whole life and then slipped up and became a total retard in a moment or if I was a retard for my whole life then randomly and unexpectedly pulled a fast one quoting Antigone and shaking off the extra chromosome? You'll be sweating and worried because you'll ask yourself "*was he playing dumb the entire time*?" and scratching a hole into your brainstem trying to figure out what my angle was.

Bingo. It's getting into the other guy's head. It's making him think about what you're doing so he doesn't focus on what he's supposed to be doing, savvy? That's poker baby! And it's people. *All people.*

In the film Hell or High Water, the marshal accurately predicts the last bank to get hit because the brothers' desperation and emotional entanglement made an all-too-easy pattern; hitting the same chain in backwater towns without a massive police presence. Didn't matter if they paid cash or they were friendly to folks. Imagine if the brothers dropped off the map, then randomly a Wells Fargo got hit in the early evening, well across town. Forget the risk and put yourself in the marshal's boots for a minute. What would you do?

For a more tangible example, when our West continues to deteriorate in the future how do you think the new 'Americans' (Mexis, Somalis, etc.) will anticipate you and your Goons to act as 'white men'? To either be cartoonishly welcoming or bitterly hostile! Hollywood is actually in your favor here because they will all think you dumb gringos who can get taken advantage of—big pale floormats who don't speak their lingo or know anything about them. *You don't have to put on an act because the White American/European stereotype as a weak moron has been ingrained in all of them.* Thanks Prejudice!

So what do you do? You let them eat right out of your hand. You can ham it up even more and confirm their suspicions—especially if you have something to gain from them say guns, gold, or food—that you're a Sucker. If they're bluffing you'll be able to spot it right away and if they aren't you just trapped them, same as if I had a Straight Flush and they had me on a King Jack. Sorry my diverse indigenous coffee bean-colored people! Maybe your ancestors will invent psychological card games after the next ice age instead of soccer with decapitated heads.

That's the funny thing about how prejudice and tribalism; you can either whine about how unfair it is or it becomes a wicked Ace in your sleeve.

BE VERSATILE. BE UNPREDICTABLE. BE A FOX.

I only really got 'good' at cards when I began thinking not in terms of 'good hands' but the importance of position and timing—idiosyncrasies of those who aren't green around the gills. And FOLDING OFTEN. Mindless potbellied gunts who stumble their way into a game of Hold'Em will make the mistake of misunderstanding their position and will get absolutely dumped on with a pair of Kings. This pudgy creature will sweat buckets, chanting 'check! check!' over and over, because he was out of position (his instinct is trying to tell him this but can't penetrate the layer between his corpulent skin and the industrial solvent running in his veins)—because all he has is a high pair and he's paying for two cards when he should have folded right after the flop! Gunt cries out in anguish as the quiet kid across the table just went over the top and bet $200 to sweep everyone with a full house on his trip nines. Gunt has no idea why he was bluffing—he just saw it on television!

GUNTING or the Gunt Effect happens to millions of people every day; they don't know how to position themselves because they are obese fat forehead RETARDS. They don't even know what a good position is or what the hell is going on if their middling lives depended on it—waddling around intoxicated with plebeian impulses like meth-addicted toddlers staggering from one hit to the next, looking forward to the Great Naptime! Cortisol and dopamine dumps every day listening to sports radio and getting fat in the head—they don't have the wherewithal or the *patience* to understand were they stand to lose/gain from where they are at in life.

This is a fancy and runabout way of saying; be lean, exploit and rob people when you can hit hard, and always have a backdoor to get out. If you're going to double down on someone or something make sure you *know* you can win.

Best guerillas in the world are ones who aren't seen as guerillas or known only as a danger until the very moment they have to attack—then slip back into the shadows or obscurity again. In this comparison to military doctrine, being out of position is like trying to hold ground or territory when you're armed with Mosin-Nagant rifles and staring down an armored division while trying to hold an outpost, like say a shelled-out building!

Consistency is key but when you're the underdog or rely on a threadbare Samizdat intel network to survive, you have to really time when you're going to raid—in poker terms, waiting to get in the best position—and that means knowing the turf and knowing everything you can about your opposition. Exact same as in Hold-Em when you're low on chips and don't have much maneuverability—a position that many of us Goons find ourselves in. It means we have to fold often and eat our ego in certain situations so we can determine when to strike at the precise time.

In literal and practical terms, it means swallowing pride and doing the soul-crushing work that earns you Trust (with a capital T, I did not fatfinger that) among certain circles or demographics, which will later pay dividends. Say you and your Goons have enough capital or equity to start a company but not everyone can be the CEO—becoming a groundskeeper or janitor will make you a loyal and dependable person. Don't let yourself be boxed in of course and know your value, but this could save you from working a 9-5 job to dip into this kind of nepotism. Volunteering for a political organization (I know, I say many times that politics is fake and gay) would allow you to meet people you otherwise couldn't to get the up and up! I have done the same but for municipal government and found out zoning regulations that will directly influence my investments—I have to tolerate boomers and their degrading gibberish, but that time sacrifice is filling my coffers!

Pride is one thing and you should never sacrifice your inner pride or ambition. But recognize that being a Goon is to be an automatic enemy of the current state, culturally, globally, and metaphysically; you are going to be out of position 9/10 times simply because you exist and refuse to keel over like a squashed bug. You don't have the maneuverability a Blackrock investor has! You must however understand that on a fundamental level he *has* to obey certain laws that restrict him from going full Slumlord Dictator—you on the other hand could perhaps ~~chum it up with the tenants of his apartment complex,~~

~~cause irreparable damage to the plumbing system with instant concrete, file formal complaints with a lawyer Goon when Slumlord refuses to pay for a hotel or fix the costs per Landlord statutes, do this a number of times to ruin the investment then swoop in and take it from underneath him~~...well this is a very malicious and obviously fictional hypothetical of a cartoon character (as are so many in this comedic novel!).

And just like in the game of spades and hearts the button will move and soon you will find yourself in position!

All it takes is PATIENCE & CUNNING!

Same as in war is the sacrality and superstitious superstructure inherent in gambling—also known as Lady Luck. You cannot cheat Her for she holds the keys to victory and defeat. Piss Her off and the heavens will open and piss on you. Win Her favor and you take the pot. The kind of rituals to charm Lady Luck may seem mundane or silly but remember that so are many in the realm of fighting and in the man's greatest art form—mortality and the taking of it, otherwise known as warfare—which is in itself a form of gambling! This mysticism which is found as far back as Rome and further involving mystical rites of fortune and appealing to said gods is not something to be overlooked.

Contrary to what outsiders and spectators believe in that war and gambling are merely realms of Materialism where we gluttonous hogs fatten ourselves on the dollar bill fields, these forms of life while offering reward also come at a high price of the external Fate that puppeteers even the masters of the games. A cardsharp is no different than Achilles where all it takes is for Lady Luck to turn her face to the shadows for even a breath to render him helpless and a mortal fool. As my readers here versed in the Illiad would point out that all the signs were there leading up to the notorious moment the immortal pirate-warlord met his demise; rites and rituals are not just for plebs! To ignore them is to think yourself untouchable by Fate.

No atheist Redditor can be found on a sheer precipice of the high Tibetian peaks. He will yowl to some God or deity to deliver him safely when his hold fails and his life-yarn is splitting at the ends.

Gambler harnessed gypsy-magic he inherited from Hungarian ancestry that made him more superstitious than a Romany crone. And as a former commercial fisherman you can only imagine what the sea has done to his internal barometer for fortune! To this day his every action is governed by a set of internal rituals like wearing a snakeskin belt and a certain color underwear and measuring whether or not his palms itch and which side to any of his ventures. We would joke and often about the pagan sacrifices needed—especially as he is a Christian but acknowledges all powers above and below—that I would make in order for him to be blessed with his favored hand; a Jack & Nine, suited.

Understand that in war and gambling to be fortunate is to still be robbing another man, Lady Luck as your witness. It is fundamentally a form of sentience and wit as you cannot play roulette with an anthill. Likewise you can play a game of dice with a cannibal islander and despite the language barrier and his desire to turn your melon into a shrunken trophy he will still understand the internal rules of Fate and will feel the momentum of the threads weaving as he sees the cast tumble onto the wooden table.

As for my own superstitions I am simple; if my luck has gone rotten I visit the lidless desert of the unyielding sun and I clean my Mjolnir in the orange sands—which will be later bathed in salt and water—and pray to Wotan and Ullr and others to send a messenger to guide me.

Seneca says and not absently;

"LUCK IS WHAT HAPPENS WHEN PREPARATION MEETS OPPORTUNITY."

Nascently (yes a play on the word) as we have seen, people are quite susceptible to mass media propaganda. In more than one way it preys upon dormant feelings or attitudes one has and exploits them like a puppet—look no further than the most Recent Thing that 'trends' (artificially likely) and sends everyone into a mass hysteria to vent their opinion on the matter. What this actually does to people is mold their brains like sponges and shave off their bullshit-antennae. With the rapid delivery of new technology systems breaking down the social order and increasing dependency on hub social centers this is an effect that will be the symptom of our lifetimes.

Uninterrupted television and social media alone has totally fried our peer's nervous systems and made them frantic little idiots incapable of even having Thanksgiving dinner with relatives they mildly disagree with. Forget even the SSRIs and the pill-cocktail the average cosmopolitan has to down so they can function throughout the day. In general the average Western person is a chemically imbalanced lunatic.

Which in your situation is grade-A.

In poker terms you are sitting down at a table of people who are drunk, are fighting with their spouses, giving their tells freely and may even slip up and show their cards. Which makes the dangerous ones pronounced but also makes your job that much easier. So long as you treat them with the same care you would with a wild herd of animals incapable of sentient thought.

As the Godfather says, a bad player can win it all if people try to bluff them—i.e. they only play when they have a good hand and they constantly call you if you're faking it. Outplay them by pure skill and temperance because they don't have that.

By almost every virtue every member of the younger generations (Millenials, Zoomers, whatever the hell comes after) are the worst players of our universe who should be robbed for existing. They brag when they shouldn't. They put everything in their lives on display. They have crippling substance abuse at young ages. They care too much about fads and fickle dogshit. They don't make plans for the future. In other words they aren't clever or subtle and if you are 75% the opposite of them you'll stand to win in the end.

What the Gambler taught me—by virtue donated some of his Alligator Blood to me—is not to be just aggressive or confident but aggressively, idiotically confident. Swagger. Put on a show. Make yourself a nuisance. Talk loudly when people are being quiet. Then take random tours veering off the reservation. Your whole act is creating an *impression* that dumb people will automatically assume is your default behavior and will not expect your subtle ruthlessness when it is time to present it.

For example I will stand at a mosh pit at metal concerts and play dumb like a stoner sometimes—which is difficult by the way with my build—and enjoy the pit. I had some Injuns totally blitzed on cheap liquor recently who mistook this behavior and when a shoving match turned into a 5-1 racial reparation match with the white kid who accidentally bumped into the wrong Geronimo. But they didn't see me come flying in to haul the kid about before he had his skull caved in. It's not a brag. If I acted like a hard-head I would have got laid out. When the knives came out me were already out of there.

Play up the image, downplay the moves.

As for the rest of the rules you should put this book down and go play some real fucking poker.

MORMON MANAGEMENT

"What joins men together is not the sharing of bread but sharing of enemies."
~ Cormac McCarthy

Old atavisms die hard—harder than your childhood dog getting run over by the drunk neighbor. We are predisposed to fill the footprint of our ancestors like rain does the track in the mud. The basis for stereotypes is in reality the contours of this ethnic 'print' contrary to the beliefs of liberal brainlets—this social history that is imprinted on every member of an ethnicity is what has distinctly formed culture. You can try to run away from your bloodline but don't forget that that which makes up your ethnicity is also a battery that powers your every movement and thought. You can't escape your genetics.

No matter my own degeneracies—from laying deep pipe in every broad in the Intermountain West, developing a gambling addiction, or fetishizing the rush of danger I have stumbled back into the limelight and by that I mean the mild off-cream Pioneer glow of my Anglo progenitors; the good old Mormons. Not completely of course or that would be very out of character for me and any of you who have read my previous work would have full discretion to harvest my scalp. Mormons are a damn fascinating people to many. A curiosity and spectacle. A crazy bunch of migratory prudes from New York, Sweden, and Germany that crossed a land bursting full of hostile injuns, imperious terrain, and barely an idea of where they were going except this crypto-Hebrew 'Zion'. Well they found it of course and the rest is history. You've heard all the magic underwear jokes.

You probably haven't heard of the reason how they've cemented themselves into the bloated leviathan of the American Financial system, how they've amassed countries worth of land, and why they're so good at running pyramid schemes. The short answer is Nepotism and they do it better than the Yids. And the long answer will be a page for you to steal for your own Goongang.

Let's get nautical and dive headfirst into a tub of pretzel Cool Whip pudding—yes...my people not only eat but relish this culinary abomination...

It's 2008 and the economy is on fire. You just had to sell your cookie cutter McMansion back to the bank along with your 2005 white suburban leather interior and told the wife you might drown yourself in Jim Beam tonight. Three shots deep and there's a knock at your door; a man and a bimbo right out of a Sears catalogue start offering you dinner for the week and talk your ear off about how you can sell oils like them to your neighbors and they sell to their neighbors and they sell to their neighbors and on. It's all white noise. You're half-blitzed and dazed as they leave your porch and peel out in a Mary Kay pink SUV.

Ye old Mormon blindside!

Curious little fact of American 21st century history; this actually happened and quite a bit. Mormons and their MLM pyramid-schemes not only thrived during the last economic recession but boomed, making several Provo all-stars billionaires in the process. It was all very simple; take a high-trust Anglo suburb suffering from financial ruin, offer them a means to make a side-hustle that grows exponentially as each member of the neighborhood attaches itself to said hustle, pushed by a group of Christians known for possessing child-like innocence, and you achieve an extremely potent business model. In a way what the Mormons and/or MLMs achieved during the recession was something to the effect of a lifeboat for certain middle-class suburbs in America, weaponizing their failing households into cutthroat vitamin salesmen.

Was it a new type of industry? No it was the oldest business of mankind and something that my brethren cut from the same genetic cloth are exceptional at; join my team or starve.

Pyramid schemes were a sociological 'macro' tribe that bypassed corporate investors, volatile derivative markets, and every other vile aspect man had begun to accept in the post-dotcom era as what buttoning on the white shirt and tie and going to 'work'. You can blame the gig economy, remote work, and the digital nomad fad all on the upside-down funnel system actually. Because it shattered the cubicle. Selling through a neighborhood was crude and effective—more than the soulless corpo could ever dream of.

Libtards clap like seals at the Broadway musical about Mormons and completely fail to recognize why the people of the magic underwear are so recognizable and influential; they have mastered human capital, small and large scale. They're better at social logistics than Comanche can shoot off a horse—they make redskins look like retards falling off of donkeys. Realize that this puts Mormons on a higher caliber than any corporation, any banking cartel, and any other group known to man that I'm aware of. Broadly speaking here but I doubt that this aspect of Mormonism can be replicated fully—nevertheless it should be attempted.

Human capital deserves its own book in the GOON library but for now it will have to reside in this chapter—because everything we take for granted in modern life depends on its ever-dwindling supply, post-Boomers. And when I speak about human capital I mean by this is a demographically homogenized community that excels at the basic framework of running a village, town, and city which is completely contrary to how your average skinsuit analyst defines human capital, which in layman's terms equates to our late-stage empire putting a metric on their parasitizing and maximizing sheer wealth they can extract from high intelligence individuals. Creating graphs that tally how many orthodontists and lawyers the system can entice into being taxable paypigs.

Human capital isn't just isolating 'talent'—high paying careers or simply bloating the button-pushing laptop caste with more bodies is what a retard thinks is useful to society—take the Mormon model for instance. FROM THE GROUND UP when a new church 'ward' building is established the whole suburb is auto-mobilized to operate its new church; janitorial duties on rotation, the bishop caste voted in every decade, women running the Sunday childcare and weekly youth activities, the men's quorum conducting budgeting and business networking, I can just keep going on and on. Mormons operate on a total high-accountability strategy that I have yet to see in any other church or business. And it goddamn works like a well-oiled machine because your temporary role as a ward member is your ticket to heaven—in other words, doing your job gets you to the highest level of the pearly gates.

But wait...there's more; if you dig into the infrastructure of Salt Lake City and how it was built, you see the same skeletal framework of hive-like organization play out in the harsh western foothills of the Rockies. Case in point look at Denver to compare. Denver was a broke mining hub post-gold rush relying solely on the mineral trade and Uncle Sam to even sustain its population (becoming a metropolis post-WW2), despite the fact that the transcontinental railroad ran straight into it. Salt Lake City which was known as Deseret at the time had no influx of gold panners, nor investors, and didn't even export its vast salt resources! No they created a massive trading hub off the backbone of good ole tribal nepotism and created what is now considered one of the only healthy cities in the continental United States to this day—despite being isolated from any coast or (usable) body of water.

It's not the funky pink salt from the Great Salt Lake or the starch in the Hawaiian rolls served at goofy ward parties—what makes Mormons so uniquely talented off of building industry and community. It's taught day one; pride in one's community and a sense of direct 'salvation' for doing the task set out for them. A Mormon man can be the ward garbage-man but also the king of his household when he walks in the door. Because instilled in him is a micro-chieftain—the only instance in our modern age for a man that marriage is worth the tradeoff of total freedom.

Show me anywhere in our globohomo society where a man or woman can have the lowliest of roles, scrubbing the filth off the gutters with toothbrushes and still be lord. Show me goddamn anywhere. Good luck; it don't exist.

Polygamy is what got the Mormons into deep shit and almost cost them the soil they staked their flag in when the US Military marched on the Utah Territory. And ironically it is only because of polygamy that they made it there.

Polygamy is what allowed the Comanche to create a giant territory where no Mexican or White dare entered for fear of being scalped or made slave. Structuring their society of female-based labor where men were free to pursue, hunt, and maximize the virility of their civilization. If not for the culling of the buffalo and the hell on wheels, we might still be fending off Comanche raids under a blood moon.

Both societies thrived in the harshest lands of the West—equally lethal environments closer to what Blood Meridian paints with a brush of human hair and blood than goofy John Wayne films of morality and goodness. You have to wonder if the strategy of one man and multiple women—giving the guy a chance to not worry about the banal household and do what he was biologically meant to; hunt, kill, and build. I'm not trying to start a polygamous cult but you cannot ignore the fact that monogamy and trying to breed men into this sort of anti-masculine caretaker type (you see these types in the newborn Christian men online) is like social neutering no different than my cucked Mormon Male archetype in GOONHOOD. It's taking your society and shooting an extra-chromosome gun into its forehead.

Men who are locked down to one woman, one household in the very artificial and modernized Christian life hide their balls from danger. They won't ride out in a blaze of glory without the wife's permission. At least with our modern 'principles' and traditions—not at all like some northman going out on raiding season, looking for new lands. Which I guess can work to your benefit in your future Goon compound; selecting these married, monogamous men and capitalizing on the chains holding them down. They won't commit heinous acts with you but they can be relied upon to build, maintain, and guard. And drool listening to your tales of adventure when you return from the No Man's land with bags of computer parts to scrap and a gang of captured OnlyFans brides.

Good husbands put wool in your ears and close your eyes for this part.

"THE WIDESPREAD PRACTICE OF POLYGAMY INDICATES THAT MANY SOCIETIES FOUND THAT HAVING SEVERAL ADULT WOMEN IN A HOUSEHOLD

WAS NOT BURDENSOME BUT WAS USUALLY AN ECONOMIC BOON. IT BECAME EVEN MORE OF AN ADVANTAGE IF THE ADDITIONAL WOMEN COULD BE ACQUIRED WITHOTU THE COSTS OF A BRIDE-PRICE OR INTERFERING INLAWS."

Tribes, Lawrence Keeley points out instinctively understood what our advanced and dopamine-drunk society has failed to; never let a good pair of hands go to waste. Which lays the groundwork for my radical idea, based on what many of my frends have said on our chats online.

Most women today are criminally underfucked, lonely, and in the coming collapse will whore themselves out to stay alive if not to feel anything. So why not capitalize on that? Don't be a fag moralist about it. Wife them all up. Only a tiny percentage of OnlyFans and online prostitutes even make money, let alone enough to pay rent. Offer them shelter in return for spreading your seed. Incredibly crazy idea I have, no?

To multiply your brood, to have an effective base of labor, to draw more to your cause—more women around you, what more could you ask for? Hell, you don't have to marry the broads. Just have them stay at your household and be your concubines. Whatever. Your other Goons will marry them off or you could use them to entice bride-prices.

Both Joseph Smith and Iron Jacket will smile upon you.

Brain drain is a cancer of the 21st century. It affects us all. It plagues the rusted iron corpse of our land where the industrial era harvested metals, lumber, and manpower for the cyber concrete jungles we dwell in now. These sub-rural areas you see in the Midwest, the Caucuses, Canada, and everywhere where the 20th century pushed whites into overdrive—creating paper tiger cities like St. Louis, Cincinnati, or Oklahoma City which lasted a frog's fart in history's eye and yet are massively industrialized.

"Learn to code" sneered San Fagsisco code-gigolos at the grandsons of the steelyard workers and coal miners whose entire career is laying the groundwork for AI or curry-stained pajeet to run the latest Wall Street tech-grifts. Very soon the arrogant metrosexual computer jockeys will also be looking for the next 'coding' or way to survive. But decades ago we were all hit with mass propaganda that every one of us will be working as a techslave while there's backlogs and waiting lists in ever city to hire a plumber—now a six-figure job, unclogging toilets. How is this?

I know I'll get hell for even saying this but going to the 'sticks will not solve your issues. Escaping the city ain't Escape from New York...yet. It is not to say I don't prefer the backcountry or one-gas station towns. I do. I'm a cowboy cookin' steak-and-egg aficionado. Issue here is twofold; most of (geographically, mileage wise) America does not produce intelligent or resourceful people and if it does they leave for the coasts and importing in unskilled swarthy people who used to worship corn demons only compounds the problem.

Mexicans do not produce engineers and surgeons who want to work in Bumfuck, North Dakota. They produce parasitic general contractors and landscapers who leech off the cookie cutter real estate industry in Arizona. So essentially an entire race of people who like cooking beans and mowing lawns. Not exactly the rocket scientists or the researchers to cure cancer huh. Oh and they're also incredibly obese so work that in too that in several decades our health care systems will be bogged down by arteries filled with beans.

Mass immigration of Mexicans into America is like

Rome bringing across millions of Africans into her walls who engorge themselves on olive oil and bread, can't build aqueducts and only hire each other to do menial tasks. Landscapers and taco-trucks don't 'build' or 'grow' the Southwest of the Great American Desert (I go more into this next chapter) which is exactly why it will return to a savage arid *Comanchería*. All purely due to gross oversight of our federal overlords who allowed the displacement of actual Spaniards and white Mormons—who turned the southern mesas into arable farmland—by millions of low-class near-slaves illiterate and incapable of integration, converting agri-compounds adjusted to monsoon rotation into arid mega-favela sprawls who rely solely on an unsustainable growth model and rapidly-depleting aquifers to maintain solvency.

Arizona is the perfect model to annihilate this empty-skulled theory that we can just immigrate our way out of brain drain and the total decline of human capital as our fertility rate of the host population (European whites) continues to worsen. Those aquifers are as renewable as liquid gold—the oil that got sucked out of the ground by those Mad Texans a hundred years ago. In fact the water is more valuable than oil, read onto the next chapter.

You and I can't solve this political landslide with our toy shovels. What we can do is harvest men and women from cities. Whether you like it or not I could fucking care—especially places with rowdy colleges. These attract adventurous people who adapt quickly and have a general lust for life. Networking with them will open doors, allow you recruits, introduce you to women and allow you to select from human capital. Why else do you think frats are still around?

Can you imagine a frat that was entirely self-sustained by its own bounties, run by weaponized autists who built underground cisterns filled with eel and shrimp farms, hacking into the accounts of the Bankman-Frieds of the world, cracking beers and creating livelihoods and families under the ground like hyper-advanced rat people—totally protected from the fallout of social implosion above ground?

If you dream it, they will farm.

"TO ME AN UNNECESSARY ACTION, OR SHOT, OR CASUALTY, WAS NOT ONLY WASTE BUT SIN. I WAS UNABLE TO TAKE THE PROFESSIONAL VIEW THAT ALL SUCCESSFUL ACTIONS WERE GAINS. OUR REBELS WERE NOT MATERIALS, LIKE SOLDIERS, BUT FRIENDS OF OURS, TRUSTING OUR LEADERSHIP. WE WERE NOT IN COMMAND NATIONALLY, BUT BY INVITATION; AND OUR MEN WERE VOLUNTEERS, INDIVIDUALS, LOCAL MEN, RELATIVES, SO THAT A DEATH WAS A PERSONAL SORROW TO MANY IN THE ARMY."

To quote T.E. Lawrence, who understood something my Pioneer ancestors crafted culturally; every man is a spiritual jigsaw in our puzzle, to lose just one is to cut off a limb. Anyone who died across the plains was memorialized and eternalized as a hero. Every man had immense value.

During the war in Vietnam we began to run out of quality men to send into the jungle to fight the natives and Washington was getting sick of wasting napalm to kill a couple rice-ninjas. So Robert MacNamara got the ingenious idea to send rejects, medical failures, and literal lukewarm-IQ chimps to the frontlines—literally throwing bodies to the meatgrinder. Which actually worsened the situation in Vietnam. Throwing more idiots at a problem is worse than throwing good money after bad—people have a tendency to emotionalize and make things very messy that abstract 'value' cannot replicate.

Something you're raised with being of Mormon stock is that one's value as acting on behalf of the church serving the 'whole'—an artifact of European migrants being community farmers with shared pasture lands perhaps— directly contradicts the Jeffersonian libertarian ideal. More or less your value to God and your family is directly tied to whether you served the community and that's not lost on any Mormon. It actually removes the shame of being a 'loser' on the individual as you are part of a group of winners. They'd rather win the championship as a team ten times out of ten rather than individual accolades—like the ESPN (Extremely Shit Pushing Narcissism) network jerking off a black guy for throwing a ball through a net so many times in a game.

People often forget that every Mormon's ancestors weren't all from the same lineage; German, Swedish, Norwegian, Scottish, and English hated each other's guts. They had every reason not to get along, much like today's atomized—in the Meatspace and online—population of self-interested r*tards.

"THERE IS NOT A MAN WHO HAS BEEN IN THIS COMMUNITY A FEW YEARS BUT KNOWS I AM TELLING THE LIVING TRUTH. DO ANY OF YOU HATE ME FOR IT? DO ANY OF YOU LOVE ME FOR IT? IT IS ALL THE SAME TO ME."

Joseph Smith might have founded, funded, and prepared the Mormons to become who they are today but it was Brigham Young who whipped them across a savage country like a Biblical tyrant and turn them into an empire. He was loved and he was hated. He was America's Moses. And what he did to ensure Mormonism would become kings of the desert was was refusing to allow Joseph Smith's progeny to cannibalize the movement—banishing Smith's children and managerial wife Emma in the heart of the Midwest. A necessary betrayal of kinds. Emma's plans had been for the Smith's to be a dynasty; to rule the Mormons for a thousand years.

What Brigham did by intention or otherwise was instill this sort of humble, frugal, plucky kind of frontier-facing meritocracy. A psychological blueprint for the people who sought the harshest, most inhospitable terrain in the West. Which is why even after they survived a financial meltdown in the mid-20th century and now are worth hundreds of billions, none of the leaders take a hefty paycheck or turn Bernie Madoff. Evangelicals across the country I would consider communist parasites—subsidized entirely by emotional blackmail via donations whereas the Mormons carefully invested and operate under the impression we still are living through the Great Depression.

Beside their social infrastructure managed from the bottom-up, talent maximization, and nepotistic ecosystem, there's one more thing I've yet to disclose. The single reason that thousands of penniless European subsidence farmers who buried their mutilated children across the plains became an empire of Aryan preppers with 100 billion plus in their coffers. Civility didn't take the Mormons from rags to ruins. It wasn't gold they mined for in them hills of granite—but liquid gold it was all the same.

Water.

BLOOD WATER

"Reason is the first casualty in a drought"
~ Marc Reisner

I am bearish on civilization and you should know that by now. And while you don't have to agree with me that we're going to be skullfucked back to the stone age, the evidence is in; the floodgates of the destruction of the modern world are being held back not just by a metaphorical dams but by literal ones—the infrastructure under our feet is eroding and their Boomer caretakers are croaking as we speak. And they ain't spending their last days fixing it—PeePaw and GeeMaw are cashing out in the Caribbean in an open relationship, being railed by mulattos over margaritas as they neglect to even mention what kind of dumpster fire they're leaving behind.

America doesn't have a happy ending—neither do most first world countries today. Newsflash bozo. The sun sets on a diabetic and dilapidated west. It's not a direct comparison but imagine if Ancient Rome was being entirely demographically replaced by a slave caste (Mexican working class), the Romans themselves were obese, constantly high, indulged a masochistic self-hatred culture, and if the mighty aqueducts were built to only last 100 years. Rome's total territory was roughly as large as the United States—HOWEVER it did not rely on modern infrastructure to operate, only in the capital and sparingly in the surrounding provinces. If America was a blonde woman in this scenario, you've dipped her in pig fat and strapped her to the hood of a semi-truck hauling out of Albuquerque on a balmy August day. Only Rome didn't have the Rockies, the Appalachians, the Great American Desert, or the Everglades—some if not all bridged by monstrous concrete roads (freeways) that have been in a constant state of disrepair even during the Golden Era of the 20th century.

Over half the country's major infrastructure has been rated at poor and almost failing according to the American Society of Civil Engineers. Wait another decade and that number will go from 40 to 60%. Another it will go to 70%. You like bridge-collapsing porn? Stay tuned! The best part is that our benevolent leaders are just throwing cash at it, which in the corporate world translates to *"we're fucked and we know we're fucked but we're hoping this big number attacks someone that can unfuck us"*. And no, China won't bail us out because they've been lying about their population and are just about to hit terminal welfare state since they over-urbanized too fast and they're having as many kids as OnlyFans harlots. Plus they consume as much as we do now—funny how consumerism is a cancer like that. Which leaves America with virtually only one country that stands to help us manufacture, offload, and control our demise; Mexico.

Except Mexicans already know they're getting the short end of the stick coming across the river—which is why Mexicans aren't flocking to mass migrate in droves, they're stockpiling land and cash in the Southwest while Somalians and Indonesians are being herded by coyotes with pills shoved up their asses. Like cockroaches, the Mexican intends to survive whatever disaster hits first; he's in it for the long haul. Props to Juan and Juanita for winning 'last man standing' award in the land where scorpions roam.

Meanwhile high-speed cartel warfare is only picking up steam with the exponential impact the flow of fentanyl has and its grip on the growing homeless and skooma-addicted American vagabond—mercenary armies run by psychopaths armed with the same tech your average Marine platoon has access to, including drones. So even if we did strike a deal with El Jefe beyond the border, you better bet that a rival cartel will use this to strike at defenseless Southwest cities or consolidate power domestically—which deserves its own book, since that entire region of the United States is fast-tracking to becoming a no-man's land where the Feds won't go unless they're heavily armored and in great number.

People often say 'shit hits the fan' which doesn't even begin to describe this pear-shaped situation—literally if you take a look at every first world's demographic and fertility charts—which will resemble something closer to a nursing home diaper-blowout and the US isn't the only one affecting by the brown tide. Trench warfare, plagues, and energy shortages have already become rampant via the Beast of the East and will spread to ape-ified Europe, which has essentially become the vassal buttboy to EU global communists. If you plan on getting a passport and taking after Hitler, prepare to either have duffelbags of cash, weapons, and a group of Goons to back your play when you reach your jungle compound. And among your Goons you better have a greenthumb, an expert in water purification, and at least one surgeon/dentist. Never said it weren't doable—just not pragmatic unless you're wealthy enough to make do.

Say you're a mule and you think I'm wrong here on my assessments—grand. I welcome the critique. Before I unload my belt-fed wisdoms here I admit I speak primarily to Americans since it's the Goon demographic. But to those of you Canucks, Euros, Latins, and other suckers from vassal countries to the greenback; this is all still of great import. America's weather is more extreme and water situation severe but your country didn't just borrow 'western democracy'; they bought the whole package. Unless Soviets built your dams—if they did goddamn you're in much worse shape than us—then your stuff was built by Americans, the labels are just in French.

Let's talk water.

We all know the West was built on the promethean backs of gritty pioneers, shrewd tycoons, and fanatical Christians. The further into the frontier and towards the Rockies called for a bolder, suicidal man. All of the rich and loamy soil was taken in the East and Midwest—immigrants were sorely disappointed to find that out when their sorry asses made it to Ellis Island. But we persevered right? Through hardship and struggle those immigrants chewed on nails, 'became American' and suffered to create life out in the wilderness on their own? By merely stepping on the ground and reading some lines on a page America was a melting pot turned into a prosperous empire come the end of the 19th century?

Wrong. Dead fucking wrong. Sounds great on paper and to the ears of boomers fearful of their own empire's shadow.

What really happened was the Civil War turned family men into mercenaries, cattle barons into crime lords, and 'good Christian men' into gunslingers. The promise of riches by gold, land, and cattle siphoned everyone from the East to the West. Racial blood feuds and ethnic conflicts were merely redefined in the fireworks of the frontier. Problem was the land wasn't arable or suitable for habitation—but in order to move iron, men, and commodities to connect the coasts, something had to give. Cities and crops had to exist to justify the trade, not the other way around. Great men like John Wesley Powell were commissioned to explore these regions for civilized expansion based on the water flows—who later was dismissed from Congress because he called them idiotic madmen drunk on greed insisting to build dense cities in this hellish land.

Remember where I was going with Mormons? Uncle Sam noticed those crazy Mormons were real good with irrigating—the only ones in fact. Save they were using snowmelt from the vast Wasatch to enrich mineral-dense soil along a small pocket of land. Uncle Sam stole their methods, federalized it into a programs and bureaus and paper-pushers and magically watered the desert with His giant flower pot so America would last another millennia.

Except he didn't.

Uncle Sam subsidized the West. He erected behemoths of concrete to hold back the natural flows, dug immense canals, rerouted rivers, and rebuilt modern monstrosities. He, the Great American Bureaucrat God thought wisely to transform this vast desert into a fertile paradise without any notion or care whether these monumental acts might have irreparable repercussions later.

Take the Colorado River for example. I have lived in 3 different states that rely on a dirty, silty, mismanaged river that is fed by snowmelt along the Rockies and snakes all the way to the Mexican coast. Over the past 20-odd years it has been choked up by silt, diverted one too many times, and overall depleted despite heavy snow and rainfall. Every one of the states under the Law of the River pact created a century ago agrees there is a dire situation afoot—but a resolution between them will never be reached in our lifetimes. Lawfare and state narcissism will talk their lungs bloody and not a single drop of water will move. 'Experts' and serial self-masturbators are and will continue to be brought out like Vaudeville clowns they are to say that the aquifer water can sustain us desert-dwellers for a time while this issue is 'eventually resolved' at a Federal level—underground reservoirs expected to sustain massive metropoli full of tens of millions of people in sprawls like Las Vegas, Albuquerque or Phoenix.

In case you weren't aware, the experts are mouthpieces to money-laundering psychopaths; there ain't no solution. Desalination costs about 3 times as much per drop of water and for low quantities of water. It can't be unsubsidized since it's a public good and there isn't a demand for civil engineers compared to bugmen keyboard jockeys at Apple. What will realistically happen? The Colorado River has been juiced for all its got and there's not a backup. 15-20 years more, there will be no more Colorado River—Hoover and Glen Canyon Dam and every other major piece of infrastructure will be inoperable. You'll start hearing a lot about 'controlled demolition' of this water infrastructure and "*How it's a* Good Thing™ *we're blowing up all the dams since it was evil Whitey who built it all anyway.*"

If you think my prediction is extreme then take a look at any of the proposed solutions to the Colorado and their estimated costs. Hundreds of billions if not in trillions that might last 50 years and requiring engineers we don't have—a comedic number considering that the Colorado and its subsequent dams alone would drain the entire funding of the Infrastructure Bill if it wasn't just padding congressmen's pockets anyway.

Nobody has the will or the desire to tackle this existential threat to the Great American Desert—because nobody is getting paid to. It all boils down to money and the will to face what our ancestors tried to warn us of. It's not global warming. It's not muh climate change. It's the Sword of Damocles made of absolutely nothing—the absence of life-sustaining waters.

"THINGS ARE FALLING APART THE WAY THAT AYN

RAND WROTE ABOUT IN ATLAS SHRUGGED. NO BIG CONSPIRACY, BUT MANY SMALL CONSPIRACIES OF DUNCES, OPPORTUNISTS, AND COWARDS."

A frend of mine wrote on Twitter, Ben Braddock.

No it doesn't inspire a whole lot of faith in what our kids, their kids, and the founding stock of America have to call 'their birthright'. Tough shit. Don't shoot the messenger.

There was this whole fiasco and chimpout with this water in Flint Michigan a few years back and how we were all supposed to think this was 'White Supremacy'—that because of red-lining or blockbusting somehow affected this poor little city's water mains, contaminating it with lead and disease. Nasty stuff. Undrinkable. Probably gave everyone cancer there. Would you be shocked if I told you that doing a little internet search for the Flint Michigan city council members yields the very fascinating results that its officers are vastly of the magical melanin ethnicity, serious felons, and a few have gone through recent bankruptcies? Doesn't take a lot of brainpower to wonder if the water fiasco had anything to do with...I don't know...cartoonish mismanagement. But wait—there's more!

Every municipality, every podunk town, every major city is a potential Flint Michigan. Mark my words, frame them on your wall. Do you think for just one goddamn second that with brain drain, mulattoization, and the continued decline of our education systems that we won't see more contaminated water? Most of our pipes and underground systems were built a century or half ago by people with double the IQ as our current city council members.

In my own town as I write in this very moment refuses to replace their water infrastructure (which is known for containing high levels of arsenic) on account of—you guessed it—the millions of tax dollars they don't have accrued for that single, costly repair. And just out of curiosity and because I'm a stubborn asshole with a curious nose, I took the liberty of investigating under which circumstances a city might fix said pipes—by asking a city councilman of my one-horse town. Know what he said? Property taxes paid for by new residents buying homes in the area. Which made a total of zero fucking sense, since my one-horse town is fast growing with gigantic suburb plats—thousands of house permits within a 10-mile radius. Maybe on paper that's how it's supposed to work if that money didn't mysteriously disappear into his and his friend's pockets.

My one-horse arsenic-poisoned town is clean by the way and managed mostly by the land-owning white grandsons of the original founders—back when it was a saloon and stable for 'just passing through' miners. I can only imagine how much more corrupt it would be if it wasn't Joe and Marsha running the place instead of JeVonteQuan and LaQuishe behind the curtain to fit diversity quotas. Probably would last a week before running out of city hall with suitcases spewing out cash as they hop into their Chrystler pimpmobile, tires squealing as they Bonnie and Clyde their way to blow it all at the casino.

You can only laugh at the corruption, local and national.

You're just the sucker downstream.

Not all land is created equal you see. I've been slingin' dirt these last couple years, learning what I can, gathering as much for my benefit as yours. Here's what I can say; the cheapest land doesn't fit into anyone's long-term solution. It's cheap for a reason. So if you can afford it—not just individually, do as the rich do and partner with your Goons or family here—and snag a land with a spring or that has Riparian Rights. You could go for a well but those cost a pretty penny; averaging about 40-50 grand in the desert states right now and the cost we're being told will only keep increasing since most are having to be dug down hundreds if not thousands of feet before they hit water. Rule that out of your bucket list or at least don't rely on it.

If you can't own it and you're poor then you need to start doing homework; map out your local area—even if you're a city-slicking Goon—pin down a good water source, then start to follow it up. Hike it. Go to its cradle, whether it's a spring or snowmelt. The higher up and purer the better. Memorize any tracks and animals that might use it as a watering hole; any of them are potential pollutants unless you like the taste of iodine water and have an unlimited supply which you don't. Water filters break down and giardia is a bitch—try hoofing with it for 17 miles with a heavy pack and over a 12k foot pass under a withering sun. Sure feels great shitting out both ends and feeling 90 years old!

This might sound all very Y2K prepper but remember that all human civilization was founded off a freshwater source, inland or coastal. Of course the most advanced cities like ours in California have rolling brownouts almost daily and water treatment plants are all on the same grid—imagine how much raw sewage will be recycled back into the taps because of outages? You'll be a sorry sonofabitch then!

But I'll take it a step further—if you have the stomach for it.

"MEN HAVE LOOKED UPON THE DESERT AS BARREN LAND, THE FREE HOLDING OF WHOEVER CHOSE; BUT IN FACT EACH HILL AND VALLEY IN IT HAD A MAN WHO WAS ITS ACKNOWLEDGED OWNER

AND WOULD QUICKLY ASSERT THE RIGHT OF HIS FAMILY OR CLAN TO IT, AGAINST AGGRESSION."

No man has more right to speak on the subject than TE Lawrence. To the Bedouins every scrap of the merciless sands was a fief—to the Arab with the sharpest sword and largest horde of horses, it was his for the taking. Stealing from a well on another's land was a murderable offense.

Fools and uneducated retards make a big hubbub about how the future of the West is a civil war, an unraveling of all common virtues over the abstract realpolitik—nothing could be further from the truth. While certain 'isms' of the early 20th century arise again and draw the lines of sand we only see war when our ability to sustain ourselves in a deteriorating empire is threatened—when bread is being pulled from children's mouths and the wells run dry. Territorial feuds over water that will make the Hatfields and McCoys look like they had a gentlemanly disagreement.

New political factions and citystates will arise around these borders. Warlords and land-barons will shore up around rivers, fords, deltas, and any tributary that can water their crops and people. As it has over our and the world's history. Potable, clean water will be the new goldrush. As such its worth will increase exponentially with every demolished dam, every contaminated lake, and silted up river.

Texas in the mid to late 20th century is a perfect example of what happens when parochial power meets the unrelenting and apocalyptic force of drought—a window into our future. Federal oligarchs threatening to seize state power, local corrupt municipalities making stacks of money disappear, giant canals costing billions (in that time) that almost never got built, stealing water from landowners, and pollution problems that worsen by the year. What for Texas had pitting homesteaders against their neighbors and allowing the Ogalla aquifer to become a cushion against a bureaucratic nightmare—a relic from the last Ice Age and non-renewable underground lake that could collapse and fill with sand—would be more violent and state-collapsing today if a catastrophe or drought cut into our systems.

I focus heavily on the West but I'll also point out that in New Orleans pre-Katrina, the levees were known by both state and federal engineers, the city was recommended and warned to build a new levee system, and there were tropical storms that foreshadowed the 2005 hurricane. Conspiracies aside there's a clear indicator that everyone who would have known about the problem did and still chose to play dumb—unfuckingbelievable. And to this day the morons have still yet to come up with a solution that would prevent another Katrina. No big shock many Whites have left that swampy shithole. The next hurricane that hits the south of Louisiana will likely cause permanent category 5 chimpouts and turn the walls of the French Quarter red with blood.

(Probably timely to mention that during Hurricane Katrina there were Blackwater mercenaries running around the flooded metropolis and all of their activities were classified—not surprising given that if you do your homework there were convenient media blackouts, ham radio was being jammed and firsthand accounts of the survivors say that the entire state turned into mini-Somalia overnight.)

I'm going to go on the record here that there's an idea I've been brewing—something I read in Against the Grain (a book you should have been reading yesterday) about a potential solution to the future of our Anarcho-Tyranny in the West and the Water Wars;

"WITHIN THIS PERSPECTIVE, SWAMPS, MARSHES, FENS, AND WETLANDS GENERALLY HAVE BEEN SEEN AS THE MIRROR IMAGE OF CIVILIZATION—AS A ZONE OF UNTAMED NATURE, A TRACKLESS WASTE, DANGEROUS TO HEALTH AND SAFETY. THE WORK OF CIVILIZATION, WHEN IT CAME TO MARSHES, WAS PRECISELY TO DRAIN THEM AND TRANSFORM THEM INTO ORDERLY, PRODUCTIVE GRAIN FIELDS AND VILLAGES."

Where is the one place in the world that you can get lost where no one will find you? Where is the place that 5G towers can no longer communicate? Where is the place that satellites cannot reliably track people? Where is there an abundance of wildlife and lack of human life? Where could Goons find freshwater, wildlife, and carry out their ~~dastardly plans~~ neo-homesteading life without being tracked down?

(cue the Apocalypse Now soundtrack)

Meet the Amazon rainforest, Vietnam, and the Everglades. I know what you might be thinking "*Claw you've gone off the reservation this time—man isn't meant to live in the jungle you mongoloid.*" And you'd be right, mostly. Except that I'm using these places as examples where your enemies (in this case, Globohomo, WEF, or simply your survival competition) cannot find you so easily. Unfortunately the mountains can be drone-striked and the deserts are too barren to support Goons. But a bogged down wetland are impassible for vehicles, nigh-impossible to survey and they boast freshwater sources that are...naturally filtered.

Natives have continued to live in isolated and

primitive ignorance in South America for this reason—it's a bureaucratic and technological nightmare to keep track of people in the boonies. And yeah it's covered in mosquitos. I didn't say it was ideal. I said it was Goon-headed and viable. You'd have to inoculate yourself somehow with the local pathogens so you don't get Montezuma's AIDS from the gay mystery-meat locals if you find yourself near Medellin. And you'd have to get to use to being soaked all the time.

But there's a reason why Muslim compounds in Thailand are still unfound and why the Seminole were the only natives in the United States to actually win their primitive wars, hiding in the Everglades; no government can tackle the swamp. They say that Afghanistan is the Graveyard of Empires. Maybe. But I say that the jungle, any true jungle, is the Unconquerable Void.

Today there's no Fertile Crescent for you and your Goons to slip into by canoe and live off the turtles and oysters but there are many wetlands and marshes across the globe that offer such an illusive option. Did you know that you can build a fully-encased cistern/subterranean hangout with cinderblocks and instant cement—easily concealable in the jungle? There's a flavor of clickbait 'primitive technology' videos you find on the internet of Indonesian monkeymen who make these elaborate mud palaces 'by hand' (comically the powertools and backhoes sometimes still in the corner of the videos) that are built and abandoned in the jungle. Despite the desecration of nature you have to imagine how easy it would be to dig a fortified bunker that collects rainwater, is totally radar and 5G proof and offers solace to the creative swamp-Goon who doesn't want to be found!

I'm just bursting full of creative and family-friendly ideas!

Grain is the other primary reason you and your gang might consider finding a wetland or somewhere with easily-attainable freshwater; salination and the collapse of the grain-based bug-civilization. Even if you don't access to these, you will need to think on your models and your access to reliable food.

To quote the infinitely quotable and apocryphal Against the Grain again;

"ARID DESERTS AND MOUNTAINOUS ZONES (BARRING FERTILE INTERMONTANE BASINS) VIRTUALLY REQUIRE DISPERSED SUBSISTENCE STRATEGIES AND CAN HARDLY SERVE AS THE NUCLEUS OF A STATE. THESE 'NONSTATE SPACES' OWING TO THEIR DIFFERENT SUBSISTENCE PATTERNS AND SOCIAL ORGANIZATION—PASTORALISM, FORAGING, AND SLASH-AND-BURN CULTIVATION—ARE OFTEN STIGMATIZED AND CODE 'BARBARIAN'..."

It might warrant you stick it out like the Afghan because the more hostile and bitter the terrain, the less pressure exerted from the ever-tightening and senile grip the globalists can put on you. Of course this means you can't grow anything or rely on the food supply chain.

I have a Goon frend I call Wrangler who manages a prosperous cattle ranch—several hundred acres and hundreds of heads of cattle. He's the exact kind of person you want to be giving tribute and gifts to allow a cow to 'disappear' into your truck from time to time (cattle are remarkably easy to maintain barring that they don't freeze and can't hop fences). Unlike the H*llywood fetishization of cattle barony like that vaudeville cornshow Yellowstone, the Wranglers of this world are actually very decent people who want an excuse to feed your Goons—you just need to take care of their needs on the backend. Bribes and hard favors are your best friend.

I may be rambling but I focus on cattle on the chapter on water because crops are DISASTROUS to the soil and consume unsustainable levels of freshwater even to an advanced civilization—I know it because my family did it and still does. Used to own hundreds of acres of fruit orchards that grew unsustainable. Beef and milk are efficient given that cattle are much easier to maintain—freeing your time and resources versus trying to guard stands of wheat.

Barbarian lands of independent cattle barons would be ideal for most of the West and even Europe given the factors of desertification and cereal monocrops permanently destroying loamy soil that our uneducated peers are overly reliant upon. There's a reason bugs and these hydroponic aberrations have been pushed recently—this is the System's solution to feeding the hordes. Plastic-born, nutrient-less FEED packaged in plastic to sallow-skinned human cattle.

And guess what? Those hydroponic farms are reliant on you named it; vastly more of our precious water. They'll drain swimming pools and siphon your 'water allowance' but they'll breed millions of sickly Tilapia and quinoa in a skyscraper to keep the masses from revolting. Tens of millions of gallons in plastic tubs under ghoulish lights in the ruins of a once-great empire, perverting the American Jeffersonian dream of owning your own soil, eating the fruits of your own fields...a dream lost to time. Could you live knowing that this was stolen from you?

To accept such a fate for your gut and your soul is one worse than death.

Thousands of explanations exist for why the Bronze Age collapse; the rapid overexpansion of empire, Sea People raiding, inflation of commodities, or just good old fashioned anarchy. I believe in another premise prescribed by James Scott; water.

Mesopotamia was looted, evacuated, and left to the sands of time when rivers began to dry up. The desert God decided their time was up. Chain reaction of aridity combined with metaphysical spirits slaking their anger upon the grain-farmers forced man to abandon his cities. I think this similar force pressured the Bronze Age cities—a wrathful god waved his palm over the land and enchanted a fruitlessness. Starvation and panic ensued, followed by abandonment and fleeing across the seas to greener pastures.

What is preventing such a perturbed divine from enacting nature's justice on us today? Forcing a long-overdue Ice Age to freeze us over? Another dustbowl from our destroyed and brittle topsoil? Or what if the temperature rose just ever so slightly—a measly 5 degrees across the board? Nothing; we deserve the judgement of a thousand different gods for the sins of poisoning the ground and erecting blasphemous silicate dildos as a big 'fuck you' to the heavens.

Be you an atheist and unimaginative kind of factory human you must still come to terms with this reality; temperance cannot last. What is considered 'normal'—a term of banal, yeasty, totally worthless connotations—is a baseline of projected hopefulness and not of any actual value. We have built our civilizations on the razor's edge—a snail on the edge of a knife, you might say. It doesn't take a pessimist to understand that anything will send us tumbling into the abyss—environmental pressures will merely accelerate what is already in motion.

The Neo-Bronze Age Collapse might very well balance on the fragile, crumbling shoulders of the promethean works of our ancestors. Dams and levees and great bridges all the limbs of Atlas, threatening with every moment to disintegrate and allow the gigantic orb of watery Chaos to pulverize man back into dust. We already see hairline fractures rippling down his spine, water trickling through the ancient concrete sculpture, pooling at his feet. You and I can do nothing to abate this collapse...what was built before is merely a shrine to a greater time that will not come again for thousands of years.

All we can do is ready ourselves for the flood.

HATCHET DREAMS; AN ENDING..TO BE CONTINUED

Two years ago I stood in an empty field and had a sort of doom-filled epiphany that if every dire prediction of the 2020, the year of madness would come to fruition, I'd be a dead man. That my throat would be cut in my sleep for being the white son and heir to the Deseret—no one to watch my back. I began to dream of wars with shadows for companions and children born in smoke. It was a strange time where the most vivid and supernatural visions were imprinted on my subconscious for no other reason than the IMPULSE of my WILL had decided I would expire and soon without my rider-or-die companions.

I *needed* a Mannerbund. More than any commodity or get-rich kind of wealth. I needed numbers. I needed ten men who were just as concerned with Blacked Lives Matter larping like Rwandan executioners. Ones who weren't weak Mormon Nerds or cowards waiting for 'normalcy to return'. If anything but for my own sanity.

Slowly I began to weed out my weak hanger-ons—my casual friends from the years I thought were these my true friends. Interrogating those who I thought would bleed and lie to the cops for me; many began to flake and show their true colors. One by one. I grew into a constant state of unease, drilling for the day I'd try walk into the bank and have my funds frozen for not injecting some evil serum into my veins, getting into a HEAT-style shootout until the bloody end.

Life in those days was spiritual atrophy.

"*Who can live like this*?" I would constantly ask with no answer in sight. Hermit-like, I began to lift weights with extreme aggression and maintained a constant feral attitude whenever I came in contact with the 'outers'; anyone that wasn't in my trusted, immediate circle. I was a recluse. My family grew accustomed and even admired my sheer tenacity—this icy, thorny shell I had developed to all around me.

And then, for no reason at all, I began to lure others in my wake. Gym-rats and loners who noticed I had an extreme rejection of the niggardly control freaks with their syringes and they voiced their solidarity. Gravitating like celestial objects to my orbit; my siren song of anger was somehow magnetizing others to my undefined cause.

A month later these former strangers and I were meeting at a park during a statewide stay-at-home order. Away from the patrolmen and the vaccine hall monitors we were talking tourniquets, grabbing beers, and grappling. Not like goofy ex-Marine get together to try to re-live their glory days in Iraq—this was the formation of a survival squad. Everyone had a target on their back—if any of us had wives or girlfriends it was on a need-to-know so we could block out our training and bonding apart from distractions.

And when the chimp-outs happened and one of our Goonsquad was isolated in the concrete jungle we were reading to react within an hour's notice. Not some retarded policing or preparing to 'defend some community'—one of ours had no one to watch his back.

Society failed the Goon but we didn't.

I've predicted a lot and projected a great deal—I can attest this is largely my primitive ape-like Goon brain bringing tomorrow's issues and boiling them down to zero-sum bones; arranging them in an ivory patchwork in the sand for you to disseminate. Even if my societal hedging is fragmentary it is a framework—a skeleton you might say. In the next decades you may not face the same issues with brown-outs but instead gangland violence, increased surveillance near hubs, and food shortages. No matter because in the end I have still provided what is not a theory but a pragmatic blueprint. And it will work.

Human networking through manipulation, bribery, marital connection, and religious fervor have bound society with a glue stronger than any ideology and for longer. Doubly so for men who seek power—aspiring chiefs and leaders. Not for title but for legacy.

"ANY MAN WHO TRIES TO BE GOOD ALL THE TIME IS BOUND TO COME TO RUIN AMONG THE GREAT NUMBER WHO ARE NOT GOOD."

I save the best of Machiavelli for last.

Great numbers of terrible, vulgar, and diseased 'men' are in abundance today. Pitiful wretches who in one breath pledge for pacificism and then jump and shriek like a hyena at the carnage in the Far East with a bloodlust not found in any soldier. Monsters driven purely by self-hate that are a shadow of their ancestors—drugged on grain slop wishing to settle ancient blood feuds. There is no religious dawn ahead on the horizon that will revert our base and ratlike cousins from their desire for 'revenge' against the West—only a meridian of deep crimson. Dear Do-Gooders; cling to your crosses all you want. Barring the son of god coming down to deliver you from this rotting and beleaguered West, you don't have a choice. You *will* join a gang on your own accord or against your will.

Revolutions, civil wars, and collapses always sway in the direction of a mob. That is an iron fact of history. Check it.

Join or die, as one American once said.

Gang up or be picked off, in other words.

I'll repeat that message—only it's not for some Anglo dream funded by the French and private financiers for a grand colonial state. One day maybe that will be available for our great grandchildren; forested hills of Goons who need not to watch their backs, living in estates of wilderness. After the smoke clears and the bullets stop flying.

No this message is for young men, for old men, drifters, and for men who know the axe will inevitably fall as it always has and always will; the hatchet. The precipice. The edge of the razor. The day when language will be reduced to the duality; life or death.

My last and final words here before I depart once more across the anvil of desert to my cave so I may consult with the gods is this; fear is the mindkiller. Be bold and audacious and seek out those who are of similar spirit. Do not settle for lessers and vermin. Insulate yourself with those who dare to question and to fight tooth and nail. They are rare but they await your chiefdom. Every day you wait to build your posse is another day you lose.

To victory and to Goons.

Godspeed my frends.

www.ingramcontent.com/pod-product-compliance
Lightning Source LLC
Chambersburg PA
CBHW051831040426
42447CB00006B/480
* 9 7 9 8 2 1 8 1 8 0 6 6 9 *